EMBRA[C...]
BY THE
DARKNESS

Exposing New Age Theology
from the Inside Out

BRAD SCOTT

CROSSWAY BOOKS • WHEATON, ILLINOIS
A DIVISION OF GOOD NEWS PUBLISHERS

Embraced by the Darkness

Copyright © 1996 by Brad Scott

Published by Crossway Books
  a division of Good News Publishers
  1300 Crescent Street
  Wheaton, Illinois 60187

Cover illustration:

First printing, 1996

Printed in the United States of America

Library of Congress Cataloging-in-Publication Data
Scott, Brad. 1949-
   Embraced by the darkness : exposing New Age theology from the
inside out / Brad Scott.
      p.   cm.
   Includes biographical references and index.
   ISBN 0-89107-900-9
   1. New Age movement—Controversial literature.   2. Apologetics.
I. Title.
   BP605.N48S39   1996
   239'.9—dc20   96-25599

04		03		02		01		00		99		98		97		96
15	14	13	12	11	10	9	8	7	6	5	4	3	2	1

Dedicated mostly to my wife, Salli,
for her unflagging faith in my abilities and vision;

to my son Evan,
for respecting me as only a true son
can respect a father;

and to my daughter, Claire,
for continuing to love me despite
my considerable flaws.

To John Hayden, Professor Emeritus,
University of California at Davis,
for straightening out my thinking when
all my thoughts and ways were even more
crooked than he could imagine.

And to Tom King, who has continually encouraged me
since our friendship began over seven years ago.

CONTENTS

Introduction: Once More into the Breach / 9

1 THE AUTOBIOGRAPHY OF AN EX-YOGI / 21

2 ONE GOD TO FIT ALL SIZES / 49

3 THE UNIVERSE: WHEELS WITHIN WHEELS / 67

4 THE MANY SONS OF GOD / 85

5 SNAPSHOTS OF THE SUN: THE RELATIVITY OF TRUTH / 105

6 A BOUQUET OF WITHERED REINCARNATIONS / 127

7 THE HOSTILE TAKEOVER / 149

8 A LAST METAPHYSICAL GASP / 171

Conclusion: The Full Armor of God / 187

Works Consulted / 203

Index / 209

INTRODUCTION

Once More
Into the Breach

A NOTHER BOOK ON THE NEW-AGE MOVEMENT," YOU may be musing, even murmuring, as you thumb through these pages. If you are, you would in one sense be right. Like the many fine books that have been written so far by such people as Walter Martin, Douglas Groothuis, and Tal Brooke, this book sounds the same thunderous warning against the diabolism of the New-Age Movement. Like those writers, I don't believe we should relax our guard in the face of its ever-advancing and escalating onslaught. In another sense, however, you would be mistaken.

This book offers something more than just a careful description and examination of the various manifestations and methods of the New-Age Movement. Attempting to break new ground, the book undertakes an intensive rather than extensive examination of the subject. Like an auger, it sets about the task of boring into the subatomic structure of the New-Age Movement: the underpinnings of its theology, its sources, assumptions, prejudices, and purposes. Specifically, it reveals how two ancient traditions, Eastern-Indian philosophy and Western Occultism, have united to form that strange new hybrid, New-Age theology. While other books have rightly warned Christians not to underestimate the influence of the New-Age Movement, this book

urges Christians not to underestimate the underlying sophistication of New-Age theology, something no other book, I believe,
has done thus far. Few New-Agers are themselves New-Age theologians, but they all nevertheless draw upon a standard set of
beliefs for nurture and comfort, just as the limbs of a tree rely
upon the taproot and its offshoots for their support and suste-
nance. This book sets out to expose and pulverize those roots,
using the sword of reason, a reason, I pray, that is informed by
the inerrant authority of Scripture, the power of the Holy Spirit,
and the orthodox Christian tradition.

Some readers may object that I have placed undue emphasis
on the role of the East in the formation of New-Age theology.
They may protest, "But the New-Age Movement is much
broader than you are representing it to be." True. But given the
intensive rather than extensive purpose of this book, I have
appropriately steered clear of counting and cataloging the many
New-Age branches. Instead, I concentrate on identifying and
challenging the shared assumptions, the common denominators,
that undergird the New-Age worldview, the roots that feed the
main, most prominent manifestations within the Movement.
The Eastern tradition is featured so prominently in this book,
therefore, because I am convinced that it's the taproot of all New-
Age theology.

The Western occult tradition from its earliest days in the
Greco-Roman world was comprised of a syncretistic hodgepodge of mystery schools: Orphism, Hermeticism, Gnosticism,
Neo-Platonism, and Mithraism. Although it's hard to say to what
extent those schools had drawn their "mysteries" from the arte-
sian springs of Eastern-Indian thought, some Western occultic
concepts have always had a distinctly Eastern flavor: the notions
that the universe is comprised of hierarchies of being, that the
nature of deity is absolute and impersonal, that souls transmi-
grate or progress through various grades of being, and so on. In
the Middle Ages, other elements were added, most notably from

Cabalism. But even then Western Occultism posed no serious threat to Christianity, partly, to be sure, because the Church squelched any incipient signs of heresy, but mostly, no matter what New-Agers maintain, because Western Occultism was too crude to compete with Christian theology for the great minds of Europe. Aside from some faint stirrings of Neo-Platonism in the seventeenth century, Western Occultism found few allies.

But something of great importance to the survival of Western Occultism occurred in the latter half of the eighteenth century. *The Bhagavad Gita* was published for the first time in English. Almost immediately, its teachings lent credibility to certain corresponding Western beliefs. By the nineteenth century the resulting new interest in the East was being fueled by such prominent figures as Ralph Waldo Emerson, Henry David Thoreau, Professor Max Mueller, and Madame Blavatsky, the founder of Theosophy. Western Occultism was further helped by the appearance of Swami Vivekananda, the disciple of the "avatar" Sri Ramakrishna, at the Chicago Parliament of Religions in 1893. While traveling throughout the United States, he made many inroads into wealthy, intellectual—often Unitarian—circles in New York, Chicago, and San Francisco. Other gurus arrived from the East, notably Swami Abhedananda, another disciple of Sri Ramakrishna, who arrived in New York in 1897, and Swami Yogananda, the founder of The Self-Realization Fellowship, who established a headquarters in Los Angeles in 1925.

From thence, the New-Age Movement was born, the seeds of Western Occultism having been endued with new life in the fertile soil of Eastern-Indian philosophy. From then on Eastern philosophy became one of the darlings of the intellectual elite, lent respectability over the years by such luminaries as Aldous Huxley, Christopher Isherwood, Allen Ginsberg, Houston Smith, and Richard Alpert (aka Ram Dass), a former professor of psychology at Harvard. And Western Occultism became a beneficiary of this new respectability. It had at last acquired substantial intellectual underpinnings for such ideas as reincarnation and pantheism. In this new climate even Western astrology, long ridiculed by Western science, could be resurrected from the dry bones of Ptolemaic astronomy. As a result, the New-Age Movement now grows unchallenged and unchecked among us.

Because secular academe, normally critical of religion, has largely given Eastern-Indian philosophy a free ride, many other fringe groups with similar beliefs—psychics, mediums, astrologers, WICCAns, paranormal researchers—have also flourished. Indeed they will continue to thrive as long as their primary corresponding beliefs are buttressed by Eastern-Indian philosophy and its formidable system of theological assumptions. Seen in this light, the New-Age Movement has acquired its glory not so much by merit as by association. For this reason I contend that if we were to surgically remove those concepts traceable to and most fully developed in India—karma, reincarnation, pantheism, the impersonal nature of deity, God as Mother and/or Father, and so on—from the teachings of Western New-Agers, the New-Age Movement in all its present manifestations would appear hollow and lifeless. Like a dead tree, it would topple, for want of a vital root system, at the first sign of a real challenge from orthodox Christianity. The New-Age Movement is indeed syncretistic, many-branched, and many-sided, but its taproot is buried beneath a banyan tree.

Although readers may encounter throughout this book some Sanskrit terms with which they are unfamiliar, I think such terms are necessary to help them understand the root distinctives of New-Age theology. Most of the terms are followed by brief translations or explanations, but two words, *yoga* and *Vedanta*, require some explaining at this point because throughout the book I rely on the reader's grasp of not only these terms but also their combined form, *yoga-Vedanta*, a term that I believe further isolates and identifies the primary source of New-Age theology.

Despite what many mistakenly believe, yoga isn't primarily a system of physical exercises. In fact, most yogis have little interest in physical culture other than to keep their bodies fit by eating well (even if it amounts to eating a wholesome American diet) and getting adequate exercise (even if it amounts to chopping wood or digging ditches). *Yoga*, related to the English word *yolk*, refers to the systematic process of practice and meditation by which a seeker of God may become united—or yolked—to God. To a yogi, yoga is the art and discipline of evolving toward perfection, attaining purity of heart, and realizing, in the end, his oneness with the Godhead. A yogi is primarily a lover of God and a mystic. Although Patanjali, who lived nearly two thousand years ago, was its main early exponent, its roots are inextricably bound up in the Vedas, the oldest Hindu scriptures, and its branches reach well into this century, bearing fruit in the form of the teachings of "God-realized" gurus, as proffered by such people as Swami Vivekananda, Swami Yogananda, Sri Aurobindo, Swami Shivananda, Sai Baba, and Ramana Maharshi.

The word *Vedanta*, which means "the end of the Vedas," refers to the philosophical portions of the Vedas, *The Upanishads*. The Vedas themselves primarily outline the laws and rituals by which Hindus are supposed to live, but *The Upanishads*, part mystical insights, part poetry, embody the Vedanta philosophy. *The Bhagavad Gita* is often considered an authoritative text on Vedanta also. As a philosophical system, Vedanta is quite sophisticated, having developed over the past three thousand to four thousand years on the soil of India, where Buddhism, Jainism, and Sikhism were also born. Of all the peoples of the world, the East Indians have to be among the most earnest and zealous about religion. For this reason, we should not take their religion lightly. They do deserve our respect.

I use the words *yoga* and *Vedanta* in combination, as *yoga-Vedanta*, for two main reasons. First, I wish to stress the point that this Eastern philosophy is both practical (yoga) and theoretical (Vedanta). Second, I wish to distinguish this religious approach, the main, most respected approach in India, from popular Western notions about Hinduism. When the reader understands yoga-Vedanta, he will realize how much more formidable it is than that superstitious Hinduism—with all its strange gods and goddesses—that commonly comes to mind and how much more sophisticated it is than the Western Occult systems that have become so intertwined with it.

In form, this book begins as a confession and testimony but soon turns into an exposé. I have chosen to include the autobiographical along with the expositional to lend credibility to my analysis and conclusions. I am not just a researcher of New-Age phenomena. As one who has escaped, by God's grace, from the New-Age stranglehold on the mind and heart, I bear the psychic scars of a survivor. Perhaps not very many Christians have been as deeply immersed in New-Age thinking, Western and Eastern, as I once was. Few who were as feted and favored by a respectable Eastern-Indian guru as I once was have undergone the radical transformation in beliefs that God has forced me to undergo. The Lord has helped me make sense of my involvement in the New Age by helping me, albeit painfully, to hack away at the intellectual roots of the New Age one by one and then subject them to minute scrutiny in the light of the Christian faith. Having plunged to the very depths of New-Age thinking and then been pulled out by the Lord himself, I have experienced the New Age from the inside out, both subjectively as a former New-Age believer and objectively as a Christian critic.

In Chapter 1, "The Autobiography of an Ex-yogi," therefore, I describe in some detail my own ten-year passage through the New-Age wilderness. As an introvert reluctant to reveal details about myself, I am embarrassed by some of the facts that I have felt compelled to relate, but I could see no other way to tell my story than to be honest. I hope that no one thinks I am reveling in my weaknesses or boasting about my sins. Although I give many details about my New-Age involvement, the central culminating event in my narrative is, as it should be, my conversion to Christianity.

In the next several chapters, the book painstakingly brings to light the errors in New-Age theology and then systematically lays the axe of the Christian faith to its roots. Each chapter details the Eastern-Indian dogmas as they influence New-Age theology and jibe with Western Occultism. The focus is on the key concepts that convince people rather than on the occultic phenomena that tend to so impress them. To this end, several basic beliefs are addressed, some of which will no doubt be familiar to readers:

- The belief that God is an infinite, all-powerful, all-pervasive substance that people may use for their own purposes.
- The belief that the universe, as governed by the law of karma, is God.
- The belief that the True Self in man is God and that ignorance, not sin, is all that keeps us from realizing that True Self.
- The belief, therefore, that all spiritual knowledge already exists within every soul.
- The belief that souls reincarnate over and over until they become Self-realized or one with God.
- The belief that all religions lead to God because everyone, no matter what path he travels, is a Son of God—a Christ, Buddha, or Krishna (in short, an *avatar* or God-man)—in the making.

One by one, these New-Age beliefs are thrown into the light of Christianity—where they are revealed for the errors that they really are—and then summarily refuted.

As the book rolls towards its close, it exposes the diabolical threat to Christianity and to society that all this deceptive theology poses, thus further discrediting the New-Age worldview. It's the final error that I expose, however, that serves as my *coup de grace*, the petard that hoists the purveyors of New-Age theology, the time bomb concealed carefully inside the trunk of the New-Age tree that at last just stops ticking and then explodes. In the last chapter, using my background in astrology as a weapon against New-Age nonbelievers, I demonstrate that the term "New Age" is itself a fabrication and misnomer. This last chapter is fittingly entitled "A Last Metaphysical Gasp—or, The New Age That Never Was." Although this chapter may seem somewhat technical at times to the layman, I urge readers to read it slowly and patiently, for it won't disappoint them if they are interested in ministering to New-Agers.

Finally, although the book doesn't propose solutions—it's expositional, after all—it nevertheless recommends in its conclusion a stance that we Christians might take. As New-Age theology continues to advance, we will have to gird up our loins and put on the full armor of Christ. With this point in mind, I humbly offer an explication of Ephesians 6:13-18. Using these sage words of Paul, I set out to explain how we Christians might start meeting this threat through loving confrontation and an unyielding witness to our faith.

First and foremost, then, I want this book to be useful to my fellow Christians who wish to understand and reach people within the New-Age Movement (some of whom may be their friends and family members) or who wish to recognize and combat the early warning signs of such errors wherever they may encounter them. I hope, however, that this book may also fall into the hands of those spiritual seekers on the fringes of the New-Age Movement who as yet haven't fully committed themselves to a New-Age path or who have felt since childhood an inexplicable attraction toward Christ, even if they have been rebelling since then against his Church or some distorted view of his Church. There are, I believe, a great many receptive non-Christians who may be nudged into questioning their uneasy allegiance to the

New-Age Movement if doubt is cast on the beliefs, motives, and methods of New-Age teachers.

My arguments, however, probably won't budge the hard-core New-Agers any more than pro-life arguments budge the hard-core advocates of abortion. I have had no intention in this book of targeting those New-Agers who wouldn't be able to sit still and read the book even if I were to coat my every argument with maple syrup. Only God can reach such people. In fact, let me warn readers now that my tone—sometimes indignant, sometimes combative—is likely to offend, if not enrage, hard-core New-Agers. The rough scars left upon my soul by my New-Age and yoga-Vedantic involvement compel me at times to resort to jeremiads and even, I must confess, delicious sarcasm. But I plead with my readers for their toleration. My righteous indignation, my prophet-like voice, proves that I am on a mission, one that I pray will help protect the Church from New-Age contagion and advance the cause of our Lord, Jesus Christ. I must be allowed to shake the tree a little. Or if I may shift my metaphor a bit, like a deft intellectual chiropractor, I must be allowed to intentionally snap the dislocated bones of New-Agers, just the right bones, back into place, if these New-Agers are at all amenable to my manipulations. If they shriek now and then, that is to be expected.

Please, however, don't do me the injustice of concluding that my sometimes biting tone is incompatible with the compassion that I, like all other believers, must feel for those who are wound up loosely or tightly in the embrace of the New-Age Movement. Any contempt that I express is aimed not at the innocent but at the irretrievably lost, wolves in sheep's clothing who proffer New-Age theology as though they were the sole agents of God on High.

Now that I have described our earthly battleground, the thesis of my book should be clear. To champion the Christian faith in a world that is almost daily yielding more and more to the

New-Age agenda, every Christian must learn to recognize the dangerously yet deceptively attractive assumptions that undergird New-Age thinking without underestimating their sophistication and influence. Mindful of these assumptions and their implications, Christians will then be able to effectively combat, individually and collectively, the deleterious effects of New-Age theology on society. Individuals as well as institutions, including the Church itself, are already under attack. And the attack is all the more insidious because many of the goals of the New Age seem so noble and benign: to help people to accept death by discovering the assurance of everlasting life in near-death experiences, to teach people self-control and mastery by means of positive thinking and self-hypnosis, to assure unbelievers that they too are aided by guardian angels and spirit guides, to inspire people to work toward world unity and peace, and so on. Christianity stands in opposition to the upside-down goals and the glib half-truths of the New Age. With all our might, we must oppose that seeming light that is really darkness.

Ultimately, however, I believe that we are battling against not men and women but a supernatural intelligence. Burrowing deeply into the natural inclinations and religious impulses of man, he endues those tendencies with a false light, distorts them, and then redirects them toward himself, promising Self-Realization and God-consciousness. We must understand, then, that we are in fact struggling "not against flesh and blood" (Eph. 6:12) but against a malevolent being who is masquerading as "an angel of light" (2 Cor. 11:14) and his "spiritual forces of evil in the heavenly realms" (Eph. 6:12). Like a Faustian familiar, the devil is enormously attractive and clever, companionable and sincere, disarmingly so—so much so that were it possible, his false messiahs and prophets would deceive even the elect (Mark 13:22). Only when this counterfeit angel of light is stripped of his scintillating robes—the yoga-Vedantic and occultic rhetoric—will we be able to discern his dark form beneath them. Only then, by seeing our enemy for what he is, will we be able to launch an effective Christian campaign against the New-Age Movement. I only hope that this book makes some small contribution to this effort.

Though our opposition is supernatural, so is our help. Without the strength and guidance of God, we can't prevail against the enemy. All our efforts to exalt the name of Christ and preserve his Church will be in vain. For this reason I have sought God's counsel in the writing of this book at every turn, aware that I am an all-too-fallible servant of Christ and an all-too-frail member of his Body.

Nevertheless, having put my heart and soul into this book for the love of Christ, I pray that he may bless my efforts for his sake and send this book forth into the world like a good seed that produces a thousand-fold yield, more abundant than the crop of any agricultural conglomerate.

May God enlighten and spiritually prosper all who read this book, believers or nonbelievers, friends or foes.

1

THE AUTOBIOGRAPHY OF AN EX-YOGI

I T WAS A WARM DAY IN LATE APRIL 1977. ON THE VEDANTA Society grounds, the turgid pink buds were bunched on the trees, and the scent of sandalwood was wafting out of the temple and along the porticoes. As I reverently followed Swami S. into his cool office with its open-beamed ceiling and quarry-tiled floor, I was soothed by the rich, dark-wood tones and reassured by his unshakable serenity. A high holiness seemed to exude from him as he stepped ahead of me, a little man in his seventies dressed in an orange Hawaiian shirt, baggy black slacks, and squeaky leather shoes. After motioning me to sit opposite him, he lowered himself into his chair and folded his hands on top of his oak desk. Behind him were rows of hardbound books on tall bookshelves—books on Vedanta, yoga, Eastern and Western philosophy. The venetian blinds to his left were half closed, like his eyes.

"Well, how are you? How is Susan?" he asked in his crisp, high-pitched voice with its clipped Bengali accent.

We exchanged the usual pleasantries. Yes, I was fine, and so was my wife, Susan. As always, I studied his dark, smooth face with its taut skin and peered into his dark eyes behind his glinting glasses, trying to fathom his state of mind. According to Hindu lore, a genuine guru is qualified to guide others because he has already climbed to the summit of the spiritual life. Having purified himself through meditation and austerities, he is forever established in God-consciousness. Although I was certain that Swami S. was a holy man, I nevertheless often wondered, "Is he what the Sanskrit texts refer to as a *jivanmukta*, a liberated soul?" At the time I believed that he was, but I always secretly wished that I could know for certain. Or I hoped he would tell me so himself: "Yes, I am constantly united with God, my divine Self." But he never did, and because of his imposing presence and inscrutable silence, I never dared to ask.

Then we got down to the purpose of my visit, both of us sitting erect and stiff, like yogis, in our respective chairs.

Since my first visit to the Vedanta Society in 1973 I had always wanted to become a monk one day. For six years I had struggled with this desire. I earnestly tried to live contentedly "among the worldly-minded" but without success. I was an otherworldly poet, an idle philosopher, an austere recluse—in short, a misfit. All that I could visualize for myself were caves and cells, holy beads and spiritual companions. I longed to spend my life in study and meditation, free of worldly entanglements—family, bosses, bills. The books on yoga and Vedanta declared that complete detachment from worldly affairs and relationships is the necessary condition for spiritual realization. Because I wanted to realize God, it seemed only logical to me that I should take the high road, the paved road, the *autobahn* to God. Why should I mark time in an illusory world of pain when a real world of endless joy awaited me in the monastery? Why should I settle for a bullock cart when I could hop into a spiritual Maserati and make like a world-class Andretti for heaven?

From the beginning, the swami had always encouraged me in my desire to renounce the world. So now when I declared that my wife and I were ready to join the Ramakrishna Order, he was overjoyed. "It is all Thakur's [Sri Ramakrishna's] grace," he said. "But first let me speak with Susan, and then I can begin negotiations with the Sarada Math in India on her behalf." My wife was to join a distant convent, and I was to live at the monastery with the swami and other American monks. There, said the swami, I would be able to use my writing and speaking skills to help him run the Vedanta Society. In fact, he went one step further. "You," he asserted, his eyes beaming like those of a child, "will be my successor!" All he asked was that we wait a few more months for everything to take shape.

Later that day I sat at home on my oriental rug in my makeshift shrine, legs crossed and candles lit, joyfully meditating. Adoringly, I gazed at the three radiant faces on the three framed black-and-white photographs before me. In the center, clad only in a *dhoti*, a loincloth, sat Sri Ramakrishna on the ground, cross-legged, Native-American-style, his eyes half open, his shoulders rolled forward, his mouth slack, smiling toothlessly. He was the spiritual father of the organization to which I belonged, the Ramakrishna Order, founded in Calcutta after his death in 1886. To Ramakrishna's right sat his wife and "divine consort," Sarada Devi, with whom he had never had any sexual relations, having renounced them in order to remain pure and constantly conscious of God. To his left sat his chief disciple, Swami Vivekananda, turbaned, eyes and mouth closed, his round face expressing both fierce determination and serenity. It was these on whom I relied each day when I meditated alone in my shrine. So now, on the verge of a glorious new spiritual life, it was to them that I gave thanks. At that instant I was smiling inside and out, swooning like a giddy groupie, overcome by love and gratitude.

But how had I come to be such a person, so willing to be estranged from all that I had known and been? How, you might ask, could a red-blooded American reared on apple pie and baseball have fallen so head-over-heels in love with such an exotic imported religion? For the answers, let me take you back to the start of my story. Only then will I be able to describe the startling transformation that was about to begin, at first as the faint rumbling of a minor earthquake and then as the mighty roaring of an erupting volcano.

THE AGE OF AQUARIUS AND OTHER NEW DRUGS

I was propelled into the New Age in the customary way—by misfortune and heartbreak. In 1970 I had one passion in life, one *raison d'etre*. I was obsessed with my former high-school sweetheart and wife of eighteen months, Claudia. Without warning, however, Claudia announced to me one day that she didn't love me and intended to leave me. And without mercy or ceremony, she did. With her departure, my world was turned upside-down. At once I began my zealous search for "the truth," plagued by questions that pleaded for answers. "What happened to us? What did I do wrong? Who am I? Why do I exist at all?"

Because as a teenager I had been exposed to Edgar Cayce, Ruth Montgomery, and Jess Stearn, gurus of the New Age, I simply acted out of reflex when the pain and confusion swept over me. I turned to the Western Occult tradition. After all, I earnestly wanted answers. And I knew that I would find them if I searched for them diligently, for it was the dawning of the Age of Aquarius, wasn't it?—a new age in which peace, brotherhood, and truth would reign in the hearts of the wise. So without thinking I shambled zombie-like down to a bookstore, found the "Occult/Yoga" aisle, and bought twenty-five dollars' worth of astrology books.

Thereafter, I devoted hours to the study of that arcane "science," with as much fervor as I had once cultivated the love of Claudia. I learned to erect natal charts and interpret the signs, planets, and aspects, using my chart and the charts of friends and relatives. Sometimes with the help of marijuana or mescaline, I would hole up hermit-like in my apartment and spend hours poring over my own chart, consumed by a passion to understand myself and the universe—to put an end to my misery.

Quite by accident, I met my first "New-Age Christian,"

Rosemary, while I was taking a philosophy class during the summer of 1970. Although she asked me to construct and interpret an astrological chart for her, she had more of an impact on me than I on her. It was she who initiated me into the doctrines and delights of New-Age theology.

Suffering as I was from grief and loneliness, I naturally found my first "guru," Rosemary, to be a benefactress. Gray-haired and dowdy, sagacious and warm, she was a lapsed Roman Catholic with five children and a tolerant, lovable bear of a husband. On Fridays I would attend her "prayer meetings." During the week, usually unannounced, I would visit her house, where I would sit at her cluttered kitchen table with coffee cup in hand, smoking cigarettes and talking to her earnestly about spiritual and personal matters. For hours on end she would patiently counsel me.

Despite this kindness, however, Rosemary did introduce me to many weird New-Age concepts. Although she claimed to be a Christian, she held that all traditional Christian doctrines are part of the old, or Piscean, age—that is, they are passé. She rejected the Old Testament, yet embraced Rudolf Steiner, Teilhard de Chardin, and *The Aquarian Gospel*, a psychic reinterpretation of Jesus' life. The New Testament, especially the Gospel of John, was acceptable to her, as long as it was interpreted "mystically." While alive, her Jesus had made love to Mary Magdalene and privately accepted reincarnation. Now he urged people of the New Age to experiment with life, love, and even drugs if they felt so inclined. New-Agers were allowed to reach out in love to everyone, even if that love was "adulterous" (as unenlightened traditionalists might have put it), for "Love" was the supreme binding force, the rationale, or rather impulse, behind all decisions: if it felt good, it was worth doing. And God, as excited as *we* were about the dawning New Age, was pouring out his love on all of us, no matter where we were or what we were doing. We all cried, "I'm okay; you're okay" and sang in unison, "Kum by ya, my Lord, kum by ya."

Rosemary also introduced me to some interesting characters. There was Jim, a young acidhead who was convinced that in a past life he had been one of the twelve apostles. He loved to make grandiose claims about his extraordinary "spiritual powers." Once when I challenged his claims, he asserted that he could "blow" me out of my chair, indeed "blow the roof off the house" and lay bare the universe for us. Oddly enough, Rosemary and her friends believed him. Then there was Ron, who always wore a black turtleneck and huge cross around his neck. Ron was homely and potbellied, but he possessed great "healing power." So potent was he, in fact, that Rosemary found him on her couch one day making love to a needy housewife. Rosemary had left him alone with the woman because he was "counseling" her. Sexual predators, wolves in sheep's clothing, abounded in those days, and few really minded. No one could judge a teacher by his fruits, for all results were relative. As long as a person was "evolving spiritually," he was free to "do his own thing."

The quirkiest character I met, however, was Dr. Wilhelm von Hausen, IV, a fifty-year-old spiritual teacher and trance medium. He was to be my second "guru." From the beginning, he affected an intimacy with me that I found flattering. During my first class meeting with him, he told me privately, "You don't need this stuff—you're far too advanced." Earlier he had been "bringing in" his guide, Zuddha, for the other students, who were actually, in his words, "just beginners on the spiritual path." Little by little, as he continued to flatter me and confide in me, we became friends, until he became my primary source for reading materials. It was he who introduced me to yoga-Vedanta.

Soon, despite the uneasiness I often felt when in his presence, I grew to have so much faith in him that I became almost blind to his faults. He was a lovable, jolly man with an eye for the ladies. In private he boasted of his sexual conquests—over two hundred of them. He had, he told me, fathered illegitimate children all over the world. I was repulsed by his crassness, and yet

I wanted so much to believe in him that I was willing to dismiss his major sins as though they were minor flaws. When I didn't respond to his sexual innuendoes—he was apparently attracted to young men also—he gradually changed his tactics and dealt with me in a more gentlemanly, dignified way.

At the time I'm not sure what I was thinking, or if I was thinking at all. Perhaps I thought he could direct me toward the truth despite his evident immorality, an immorality that I later learned had extended, by his own admission, to the sale of pornography, a swinger's lifestyle, and even the sexual abuse of his children. Whatever I was thinking, I hadn't as yet learned that a teacher can be judged by his fruits. I couldn't discern that he was a false prophet—outwardly a teacher, inwardly a ravenous wolf. I saw only a learnéd man, a psychic, a true spiritual seeker. Perhaps I sensed that I was flirting with danger, but I felt, for the most part, safe.

Obviously, then, I was convinced that my spiritual life was thriving. In 1971 I taught astrology classes through a university's "Experimental College" and interpreted people's birth charts for the "noble purpose" of mitigating their suffering and contributing to their self-knowledge. During this time also Dr. von Hausen was introducing me to the many yoga books in his library: *The Autobiography of a Yogi* by Yogananda, a biography of Sathya Sai Baba (a so-called modern avatar), *The Yoga Aphorisms* of Patanjali, and the *Vivekachudamani* by Shankara. All of these turned my head around, as Wordsworth once put it, "as with the might of waters." But Shankara's book especially filled me with awe and inspired me to venture boldly into still newer spiritual territory.

From February to August of 1972, I responded to this new philosophy by making several changes in my life. It was a time marked by austerities and self-discipline, by what I now call "a macho spirituality." To free myself from various "attachments" to my body and mind, I quit listening to rock music and stopped drinking alcohol. Although I had only been a casual user of drugs, I began to say no to my friends. I even began to control my sensuous appetites by examining my thoughts and actions for signs of selfishness. At last I had found my royal road to liberation. I could escape from my pain and guilt—from myself—by seeking a Truth that was above my senses and required their complete subjugation. "*Aham Brahmasmi* (I am Brahman)," I eagerly intoned, aping the words of the Hindu seers. "In my true nature, at the core of my being, I am that absolute Truth."

Oh, how I began to swell with conviction! I was on the march—bound for the ranks of the spiritually smug.

A PILGRIMAGE TO INDIA AND OTHER BAD TRIPS

After T. S. Eliot became a Christian, he wrote, "The last temptation is the greatest treason / To do the right thing for the wrong reason." A living testimony to his observation, I ardently pursued "the truth," aflame with a desire to escape from all that I had been and done. And I was prepared to undergo any disciplines and travel to any locale on the globe to achieve it.

For the next year I bent all my efforts toward practicing austerities and meditation. I was trying to purify myself and so prepare myself for union with God. To this end, I arose at 5 every morning and sat on a bare wooden floor before a candle, wrapped in a threadbare blanket, reading yoga books and meditating on my Supreme Self, the godhead within me. Despite the discomfort, I refused to yield to my body's demand for the warm blankets, soft bed, and luxuries of prolonged sleep. Again and again I redirected my mind, with the force of my will, back to the object of my meditation. Sometimes, as demented as it may sound, I would even slap myself in the face. The sting would frustrate my longing for comfort and reawaken me to my purpose. And the tingling that lingered on afterwards served as a reminder that my body and mind had best behave or suffer further deprivation. But most difficult for me was the renunciation of sexual intimacy. To accomplish this feat, my future wife and I slept in separate rooms. We weren't always successful, but I suffered a great deal. At the time, I'm sure, I believed that suffering for a good cause was almost the same as succeeding in it.

To make such self-denial all the more meaningful, I continued to read everything on Vedanta that I could lay my hands on. Gradually I remade my mind in the image of Eastern philosophy. I understood the three main systems of Hindu theology: *dvaita* (dualism), *vashishtadvaita* (qualified non-dualism), and *advaita* (non-dualism). As taught by *The Bhagavad Gita*, I sought to harmonize the four yogas: *jnana* (knowledge), *raja* (meditation), *bhakti* (devotion), and *karma* (work). I acquired a stock of Sanskrit terms that helped me rationalize my new worldview. I became puffed up and vain, even about my newfound humility: I was nothing; Brahman was everything. (But, of course, in my real nature I knew that I *was* Brahman.)

Nevertheless, I still lacked one thing: a guru. "When the student is ready," the books declared, "the teacher will appear." And of course I was sure that I was ready, if eagerness can be equated with readiness. In those days I felt drawn toward Sai Baba, an avatar (incarnation of God) and miracle-worker. I assiduously studied his books and built my shrine around his image. Born in 1926, he is a short but handsome man who sports an Afro and wears, as his trademark, a full-length, red-orange robe. He smiled at me from his pictures and held forth the promise of spiritual fulfillment. I felt drawn to him because as an avatar he was supposed to be omniscient and omnipotent. He heard my prayers and responded to my needs, so he and his followers claimed. On several occasions his devotees in America had even reported that sacred ash had fallen from his photographs onto their tables, further confirming his divine mission. Sai Baba had even referred to himself as the Comforter mentioned by Jesus and the spirit of truth mentioned in Revelation, he who rides forth on a white charger to rid the world of evil (Rev. 19:11-16).

So in January 1973 Susan and I decided to visit India in the summer to commit our lives to this holy man. In the meantime, in March 1973, we met Swami S., who was to become my last guru. From March until June we attended his classes on *The Bhagavad Gita* and Sri Ramakrishna (1836-1886), another avatar. At the time we couldn't wholly commit ourselves to Sri Ramakrishna, even if he was an avatar. Our hearts already belonged to Sai Baba. Besides, India, it seems, is full of avatars. Because we had already read or heard about many of these avatars, compared them with Sai Baba, and found them wanting, we weren't prepared to shift our loyalties easily.

In June I received my M.A. degree in English, and Susan and I married so that in our travels through India we might be a proper couple, less likely to raise eyebrows. In August, excited and hopeful, we boarded a 747 bound for India, the "Holy Land" at the time for the disenchanted and irresponsible young. We were prepared, if necessary, to remain in India for the rest of our lives to serve Sai Baba. If he were an incarnation of God, we reasoned, we would be foolish to do otherwise. Like Jesus Christ, he would have the power to make us "new creations," to liberate us from *maya* (our illusions and delusions) and lead us into union with Brahman.

Fortunately, the trip was a fiasco. Everywhere we encountered heart-rending, grinding poverty. I shall never forget the painful images of pleading mothers balancing runny-nosed infants on a hip with one hand while begging with the other; or of ragged boys riding on flea-infested trains apparently going nowhere; or of the miles of cardboard and clapboard shanties along the modern highway leading into Bombay. In Puttaparthi itself, the site of the ashram, we were ignored, both by ashram officials and Sai Baba himself. Later, in Bombay, on our way home, we were robbed of all our traveler's checks. And once at home in the

United States, I came down with a case of dysentery that was to last for six months as a grim reminder of my "holy" trip. In this way, painful as it was, I got Sai Baba out of my system. (Anyone wishing to know more about this Svengali of a swami is encouraged to read Tal Brooke's book *The Lord of the Air*, which provides much more detail about this man and his ashram than I can provide in this brief chapter.)

A few months after our return, after secular setbacks and a case of pneumonia, I took stock of my spiritual life again. For two years I had spent one year arguing mentally with Rosemary and another year exorcising Dr. von Hausen from my mind. Now, with Sai Baba knocked off his pedestal, I was prepared to settle down and follow one guru. Because I was impatient for success and Swami S. was conveniently located in my hometown, I felt that it must be the will of God that we attach ourselves to the Ramakrishna Movement.

THE GURU IN GERUA AND WING TIPS

From then on we became regular visitors to the Vedanta Society, a compound located on five acres in a suburb of Sacramento. A solid fence, six feet high and tan, enclosed the grounds, preserving the illusion that everything within its precincts was holy. Just inside the fence, from left to right, were the swami's apartment, office, and library and the monks' quarters. Behind the swami's quarters was a large patch of sloping lawn. Behind the monks' quarters was the "Temple," as the devotees called it. Actually it was an inoffensive-looking monastery-style church, complete with plain windows on either side, neat rows of chairs, a central aisle, and an altar at its far end.

Like the compound itself, the area behind the compound was meticulous, a testimony to the fruits of karma yoga—namely, the labors of the swami's devotees. It consisted of a flower garden and landscaped sections devoted to Hindu saints: "Krishna

Pond" with its life-sized statue of Krishna, the Guru Nanak Shrine, and so on. Because every graveled footpath led to some landmark or shrine devoted to God, a casual visitor would naturally conclude that every spiritual path was respected at the Vedanta Society. There they worshiped a large-hearted, all-embracing God—just the kind of God that my wife and I had been seeking.

Ah, yes, we had found our spiritual sanctuary at last.

Normally Swami S. wore comfortable American clothes—slacks, polo shirts, sports coats. But when he presented himself as a teacher, he wore *gerua*—the bright orange robe of a monk—over his street clothes, revealing only his socks and wing tips beneath. When teaching inside the Temple, he stood still behind a podium or sat regally in a high-backed chair on a carpeted dais, his dreamy eyes sparkling, revealing yet concealing his profound spirituality. Behind him was the recessed altar, a long table with candles and flowers on it, and above the altar pictures of Buddha, Swami Vivekananda, and Jesus Christ. The message was clear: at this altar all great religious leaders are worshiped and honored equally. "*Ekam sat vipra bahudda vadanti*," declared the expounders of Vedanta: "As many faiths, so many paths."

Our early visits exposed us to the benign public image of the Society and indoctrinated us into the basic teachings of Vedanta as they appear in *The Upanishads* and *The Bhagavad Gita*. Publicly they honored all paths and "incarnations of God." They weren't seeking to make converts but only to promote the truth: all religions are one; there is, despite appearances, only unity in diversity, only harmony everywhere—for those enlightened enough to see it. This harmonious vision was the answer, they implied, to all the world's problems. Religions and nations had no reason to quarrel. Every religion—indeed, every path—led to the same God. Manliness, grit, self-reliance—these were the only virtues required of those benefactors of mankind who would embrace and apply this vision. Swami Vivekananda, Rama-krishna's chief disciple, put it best:

> Do not seek help from anyone. To feel helpless is a tremen-dous error. We are our own help. If we cannot help ourselves, there is none to help us. "Thou thyself art thy only friend, thou thyself thy only enemy. There is no other enemy but this self of mine, no other friend but myself." This is the last and greatest lesson and oh, what a time it takes to learn it.
>
> —*Sayings*

Ralph Waldo Emerson couldn't have put it any better: self-reliance, the American creed.

The private side of the Vedanta Society, however, was a dif-ferent matter. Until we were initiated as Swami S.'s disciples, we remained outsiders, ignorant of the attitudes fostered by the swami and his inner circle. After our initiation we were admitted more and more into the inner circle of devotees, a core group of about twenty-five who had easier access to the swami. Soon we were visiting the Vedanta Society five times a week. Soon, like the other devotees, we believed that the Vedantic answer was the only answer. It was so broad and inclusive, so tolerant and inof-fensive, so very logical and coherent. Like them, we too had opted for the broad and best way. Our *Ishta*, the personal form of deity we worshiped, was now Ramakrishna. Our guru, the divinely appointed guide who knew all there was to know about us, past, present, and future, was Swami S.

But membership in the inner circle had its price. Relationships that might have elsewhere flourished were marred by envy and mistrust. Devotees, secretly coveting the little crumbs of affection that the swami doled out, discreetly competed with one another for his attention. Some jockeyed for opportunities to be alone with him; others, like strutting peacocks, displayed their "holi-ness" at every turn. One devotee, for example, once boasted to me that he hadn't slept with his wife for over a year and that she was a saint because she performed thousands of *japams* (repetitions of her mantra) each day. Another devotee, a young woman who was preparing to become a nun, loved to lord her favored status with the swami over the rest of us. Because she spent more time alone with him than anyone else, she felt that she could treat the rest of us as she pleased, grousing and stomping around the premises in a snit whenever she didn't get her way. But none of us "householders" dared to correct her. That, we knew, was the swami's job. After all, he alone knew what was best for each of us. So we bit our tongues and practiced forbearance. Unbeknownst to us, we were all actors in an Eastern-Indian drama called *Swami Knows Best*.

And the old swami—as unassuming, emotionally detached, and serene as he seemed to be—had his hand on all our spiritual and secular lives. Young and old sought his advice. Daily they would disappear with him behind his office doors, where they would pour their hearts out to him. "My husband has sex with me all night like an animal. What can I do?" went one report, according to gossip. Or, "Should I accept this new job, Swamiji?" I, too, sought his advice in both spiritual and secular matters. Most of his secular advice, however, was too general or noncommittal to be of much use. "Yes, yes, I see," he might say. "Well, that's all right if you want to do that. As a yogi you can do any kind of work. It won't hurt you [spiritually]."

At home, between 1974 and 1976, my wife and I lived like otherworldly hermits, so much was I intent on being the perfect yogi. In fact, "Yogiraj" (yogi-king) was the name that the swami had given me. To live up to his high view of me, I followed all his advice without question. My wife and I decided not to have children because the swami had warned us that they would "ruin" our spiritual lives. I forsook old friends and strained my relations with my family because I had learned that meditation is more important than communication. I was a little spiritual world unto myself. Already, in my dreams, I lived alone among the hills in a cave, where I studied and meditated. In my real world no one else, I assumed, had anything else to say to me about the truth. I had found it. For the time being I simply had to endure the world. I had to remain "a hidden yogi" until I could cast away the world like a crumpled candy wrapper.

Yes, oh, yes, I was at last on the high road, the fast track, the *autobahn* to God.

HINDUIZATION AND THE NEW DOGMA

By 1976 my wife and I had fully embraced our imported religion. As members of a singing group, we spent hours learning Bengali devotional songs; we sang at *pujas* (worship ceremonies) and traveled with the swami to perform for the devotees of Ramakrishna in other cities; and we sat in *chaddars* (shawls), swaying with the other singers to the sounds of the harmonium, tampura, and tablas. "*Prabhu misha manisha,*" we sang while the swami and the other devotees meditated on their True Self or swooned in silent ecstasy. Although we had resisted this Hinduization at first, we found that the closer we drew to the swami, the more we had to forsake our Western perceptions. The inner circle, if not the swami, demanded it. After *pujas* we would loiter around the swami's apartment, lingering in his living room with the other devotees, waiting for him to finish his Indian cigarette and shuffle out of his bedroom, glassy-eyed. If he said, "Chalo, go home—it's late," people would meekly bow their heads, smiling conspiratorially at each other or silently studying their hands. But they wouldn't go home. They waited for the swami to sit in his armchair. Someone would try to get him to talk or sing.

Gradually he would submit to the wishes of the devotees. In part, they wanted to hear him speak, but mostly they wanted to touch his feet and receive his blessing. Some courageous soul would be the first; others would follow, kneeling before him, touching his feet with their fingers and foreheads, taking their leave of him but not leaving. Afterwards they would remain standing or sitting, hands folded, waiting for his general dismissal of us all. Relaxed among his intimates, he would laugh and tell special stories about the Ramakrishna Order that were reserved only for the ears of devotees. And all those around him would be "high" on holiness, giddy or solemn, exuberant or shy. Through the swami's love, we were bound together. We were his.

During this time also, the swami decided that I should join his other "platform speakers," academic types handpicked by him to speak to the congregation on Sundays in his absence. After all, he kept telling people that I was a philosopher and poet. He had to know what he was talking about, right? He was, after all, the guru, the one person in the whole world who truly knew me. So on different occasions I confidently mounted the sacred dais and spoke about the Vedanta philosophy before seventy-five to a hundred devotees and visitors. By bestowing this honor on me, by respecting and trusting me, the swami had paid me a great compliment. By now I had ample evidence that I too was most certainly his.

Under the swami's influence, my life had taken on new meaning. I had become special by being specially blessed by a holy man. Among billions of people, I had been fortunate enough not only to secure a self-realized guru but to have as my savior an avatar of the first magnitude, one who guaranteed my liberation from the insipid world in which my karma had forced me to live. At the Vedanta Society, even if nowhere else, I was a great spiritual seeker. There I could receive my spiritual fix from the swami, devotees, and surrounding environment, with its ambiance of certitude engendered by its perennial flowers, multi-sectarian shrines, and curving graveled pathways that always led a wanderer away from and then back to the monastery-style Temple. As long as I remained loyal to the Vedantic ideal, I could number myself among the Chosen People. When the people outside the Temple precincts were ready, perhaps in a week, perhaps after a thousand lifetimes, they too would come around to the Vedantic way of thinking. In the meantime, if they desired consolation they would have to make do with their personal God and "comfortable religion."

In every respect, then, I was a textbook Vedantin. Even my spiritual experiences conformed with the textbook descriptions. I often felt the warm thrill of the *kundalini*—the life force that brings enlightenment—rising up my spine, intensifying as it reached my stomach center and then my heart center, expanding my consciousness, empowering and delighting me. And then when I mentally pushed it upward toward the crown of my head, I felt a few times as though I had merged with an all-encompassing light. The joy and peace were overwhelming. Sometimes when I was meditating on pure Being, my body would seem to fall away from me and my thoughts would cease, my whole sense of self becoming attenuated. I was no longer Brad Scott. I simply *was*, because Being alone was—Being and nothing else.

Daily I reminded myself, as the books on *jnana* yoga insisted, that I wasn't my body, mind, or ego. I was pure Being. I was the Self. Yet my circumstances constantly reminded me that I had a body, mind, and ego. When my toilet was clogged, I had to ask Dad to bring a snake over and unclog it. I had to deal with nasty little details. When I was exhausted by my studies or austerities, I parked myself before the TV and happily watched *The Rockford Files*, forgetting God and feeling good. And when the pettiness of coworkers got to me, I grew edgy, then angry, then intolerant of all the sham. I wanted to quit work, to flee to my shrine and sit on my meditation cushion, dreaming of the monastic life, concentrating on the *kundalini*, on infinite light, on Sri Ramakrishna. I wanted Liberation! Yet no matter how hard I tried, I couldn't escape my sense of self.

Everywhere I turned I experienced *I*, *me*, and *mine*. And as hard as I struggled to acquire patience and humility, I was sick unto death of myself.

At the same time, at the prompting of the swami I read the books on *bhakti* yoga to develop my devotional side. "Love," the swami said, "is the way to Truth. Too much asceticism makes the body take revenge." By now my immersion in yoga-Vedanta was such that I could embrace the devotional practices of the other devotees. Like them, I could gaze at Ramakrishna's picture, speak to him during prayer, and imagine his smiling form in my heart. Like them, I could joyfully attend *pujas* and sing Bengali songs. Like them, I could touch the swami's feet, all atremble inside, believing that his love for me was greater than any I had ever known. With all my heart I strove to be simple and humble.

The books also promoted karma yoga, the yoga for workers. Again at the prompting of the swami, I studied the books. I strove to dedicate all my thoughts and actions to God, surrendering their fruits, good and bad, to God, serving God in man, recognizing that God alone is the "doer," as taught in *The Bhagavad Gita*. I tried to maintain my equanimity while being praised or blamed, while experiencing pleasure or pain. My life was a dewy gardenia that I was offering up to God. Its fragrance was my love; its moisture, my tears; its milky whiteness, my purity of heart. I only asked that God would use me for his purposes.

At home this practice was easy enough when I was alone. To remain in the right frame of mind, I could read only spiritual books; I could write only devotional poetry. And so I did. I crammed my head full of Hindu terms. I wrote stilted, abstract poetry on Vedantic themes—on renouncing the body, worshiping Ramakrishna, realizing the True Self. But when I snapped at my wife or allowed the fallen apricots in my yard to pile up, I didn't find it so easy to sacrifice the fruits of my work to God. When those fruits seemed rotten or defective, I couldn't help feeling responsible for them. And when I did, I had to call them my own; I then had to rectify *my* behavior. So there was that curséd "I" again. There again was my failure to remember and obey God at all times. So I shrank from work, felt uneasy about it, yet secretly hated myself for my cowardice.

Nonetheless, I had always wanted to be a college instructor and writer. But these careers seemed closed to me—first, because there were few, if any, community college positions available after the Viet Nam War had ended, especially for inexperienced teachers; second, because I could only see myself producing unmarketable books and articles on "higher topics" for which almost everyone was unprepared. I was just too specialized, I felt, for life in the world. I didn't fit. I was stuck.

Therefore, I could only reach one conclusion: I had been fitted by God for monastic life. As a monk I would be able to fulfill my dreams and find my true place in that sheltered, spiritually-charged world. I would be able to study, meditate, write, and even teach, speaking before the congregation on spiritual matters—not at first, of course, because Swami was the teacher and I was the student. Even though seven years of training awaited me before I would be qualified to become a *sannyasin* and earn the title "Swami," I was willing to wait and serve.

Meanwhile, I kept building my own tower of Babel, bolting down the girders, moving deftly along mile-high catwalks. I perceived no dangers. I revered the ancient Vedantic tradition and trusted my guru. Thousands before me—slender, dark-skinned meditating ascetics in turbans and loincloths—had successfully ascended to God by the Vedantic route. They confirmed and validated my experiences. I was certain, then, that the renunciation of worldly relationships and affairs was the most logical course for a true lover of God, for one who sought liberation from the interminable rounds of births and deaths—in short, for me.

THE UNEXPECTED LIBERATION

Now, full circle, I have arrived at the beginning and ending of my story. In the summer of 1977, as I sat swooning in my shrine after my interview with Swami S., I felt nothing but joy and relief. I could now devote my whole life to God alone.

But the motions of the spirit are indeed strange. Only three days after the swami had declared that I would be his successor, something unaccountable began to occur. From within me an "alien" power too deep for words suddenly began to rock the foundations of my faith. As an indefinable yet frightful anxiety, it seemed to be burrowing into the very ground of my being, rattling loose as it did so the steel bolts of my spiritual edifice. Soon my interior life was erupting, Vesuvius-like, in chaos. My journal from that period describes the intermittent prostration and doubt that I was enduring: "I'm beginning to doubt my fitness for monastic life. How can I ever be pure or perfect enough to be Swami's successor!?" By July I was overwhelmed by a fear that something was terribly wrong. When the forces of flight or fight began to clash, it was flight that won.

In August, four years after earning my M.A., I hastily reapplied to graduate school to work on a doctoral degree, not so much to become a scholar as to confront the world from which I had been fleeing for years. In reality, however, I had only taken refuge in another monastery, an academic one, so that I wouldn't have to confront my raging doubts about the yoga-Vedanta monastery from which I was now fleeing, frantically seeking cover like a crazed man in a bath towel racing out of a burning high-rise.

But my escape was no escape at all. I couldn't flee, it seemed, from that inexplicable, insistent, alien power that was searching and upbraiding me, challenging the only spiritual life that I had known for six years. Before its onslaught, my yogic self-control meant nothing. With my mind as disturbed as it was, I also faltered in meditation. Although I still faithfully visited the Vedanta Society, I did so with a difference: I was now ashamed because I felt that I had been unfaithful to the Vedantic ideal. So I began to slink around the place, afraid to encounter the swami. I had fallen from grace. My spiritual ship had been wrecked on the shoals of worldly ambition. Even worse, I had lied to myself—or been lied to—about my spiritual aptitude. I was no longer fit to be a lowly monk, much less an enlightened guru's successor. The psychic turmoil evoked by my visits soon became too much for me to bear. With each visit, my cheeks grew redder, my breathing more labored.

To make matters worse, my studies were so demanding yet fascinating that I had little time to think of anything else, much less meditate on my True Self. I was a bundle of nervous energy, driven by desires, ambitions, and various vexations. I would only find peace when I would lose myself in my research, following a thread of knowledge as far as it would take me, challenging old theories, considering new ones. Had Wordsworth really lost his nerve, as the critics claimed, when in later life he became a conservative, a Christian, and the Poet Laureate? What was Eliot attempting to do in his *Four Quartets*? What influence did Augustine's *On Christian Doctrine* have on literary theory? Are all judgments merely relative, or are there absolute criteria by which we can make decisions?

Unable to sit still for meditation, much less calm my agitated mind, I turned in desperation to prayer as my only hope, seeking consolation from Ramakrishna, fully convinced that he would comfort and guide me. I kept recalling Ramakrishna's analogy of the kitten that can only meow and meow until its mother rescues it, picking it up by its scruff and whisking it off to safety. The devotee, he said, is like that kitten—helpless, totally dependent on the grace of the Divine Mother. With great fervor and faith, I would pray, rocking back and forth, the tears streaming down my face, waiting for Ramakrishna to rescue me. For fifteen months I continued in this way, and still I received neither consolation nor light. Meanwhile, I continued to avoid contact with the swami, partly out of shame, partly out of an irrational fear of rejection and ridicule.

Actually, as time passed I began to realize that this fear wasn't groundless at all. For a long time I had regarded the swami to be infallible—pure of heart, perfect in judgment—ignoring or excusing his unpleasant side. The swami, I now began to recall, had always been a harsh taskmaster. I remembered the times during our Saturday night class when he had directed a devotee to show uninvited visitors the grounds, confiding in us as the door closed behind them that they were too "worldly-minded" to experience the spiritual delights of which we were about to partake. He had no patience with people who weren't "ready" for higher teachings. I had heard him criticize married devotees for having children. To their faces he would say, "You can still have a spiritual life. Just mediate on your child as Krishna." To me he would say, his lip curled in disdain, "Their spiritual lives are ruined." I had heard him relate the failures of former devotees as anecdotes, long after they had left the Vedanta Society. I had even heard him, as refreshments were being served after a *puja*, call a woman of his inner circle a "dumb bunny" because she wasn't moving fast enough to suit him. If he was trying to be cute, believe me, nobody was laughing. Servers began to scurry even faster with their trays.

At last, in August 1978, I worked up the nerve to invite the swami to visit my wife and me in our home. While there, however, he made no mention of my previous plans to renounce the world. He simply offered us the same old methods. Chant Sanskrit hymns, sing Hindu songs, do *japam*, he told us. Methods—always more methods; but where was the comfort and reassurance I so desperately sought and needed? Admittedly, I put his guru's "omniscience" to the test, waiting for him to help *me*, the person. But he failed. Either he refused to acknowledge that I was a person with real feelings and needs, or he simply didn't know me at all: he couldn't really see into the heart of his own disciple.

By December 1978 my suffering was acute. By then I was challenging Ramakrishna: "If you're real, if you have any power at all to save your devotees, then you must save me now!" But there was no response. It was as if I had cried out in the dark desert of my soul but then, after pausing to listen, only heard an icy wind whistling across the barren plains in response.

Then the unexpected took place.

As every good Vedantin, every good follower of Ramakrishna, did every December of every year, I was preparing myself for the birth of Jesus Christ. At the Vedanta Society, Christmas was conscientiously observed. A Christmas tree would go up in the library, devotees would exchange Christmas presents with the swami, and a choir of Vedantins would practice traditional carols for the forthcoming celebration of Jesus' birth. On the Sunday nearest Christmas, all would gather to sing carols and hear the swami explain just how Vedantic Christ really was, how universal and undogmatic he was. At home I observed Christmas by trimming a tree and rereading the Gospels during my meditation hour.

This particular year I certainly didn't expect to encounter the *real* Jesus Christ while sitting cross-legged in my shrine re-reading the Gospel of Luke. But when I came to the story of the sinful woman who bathed Jesus' feet with her tears and then dried them with her hair (Luke 7:36-50), I was suddenly struck so hard by the unparalleled beauty of God's unconditional personal love that my whole spiritual life was turned upside-down. I identified with her sorrow, her longing to be forgiven, to love and be loved divinely. I especially understood her self-abandonment at the feet of Jesus, having myself reached the limits of my endurance. When Jesus said to her, "Your faith has saved you; go in peace," I heard him speaking to me and went limp inside. Instead of feeling a *kundalini* power rising up my spine, I felt a warm sensation descending from the top of my head down, sliding slowly down like chrism, anointing me as it flowed down into the depths of my subconscious mind, as it were, to the bottom of my soul and then welling up again as though it were coating the insides of an empty vessel. The Word that entered me, the words that entered me, seemed to be saying, "I love you personally, you, all that you are and all that you have been, all of you now and forever. And know this, too, my child, Bradley E. Scott: once and for all time, you are mine and I am yours."

Until this moment all my former spiritual experiences had seemed real. Now they paled into insignificance. Never before had I experienced such comprehensive, unconditional love. Never before had I been *touched* by God. In all my searching, I had worshiped what I knew not and, by my own efforts, had touched what I thought was God. But now God, the one and only true God, had searched me out and embraced me wholeheartedly, as wholly unworthy of him as I was. Even now as I write these words, I know that there isn't a Vedantin or New-Ager alive who will understand what I'm saying, except by labeling it as dogmatism or parochialism, unless God opens his or her eyes and heart. In my defense, sad to say, I can only invoke the words of Jesus: "He who has ears, let him hear."

Soon afterwards, I was struck also by the contrasts between Ramakrishna and Jesus Christ. For one thing, unlike Jesus, Ramakrishna would recoil, shrieking, from the touch of a "sinner," even a penitent sinner. He was so pure, the rationale went, that sins literally burned his skin. His disciples, therefore, were careful to protect him from the entreaties of sinners. For another thing, again unlike Jesus, Ramakrishna lived safely sequestered on Temple grounds, only venturing forth with his entourage of devotees. He never moved lovingly among the masses of Calcutta, healing and forgiving them; he catered, instead, to the spiritual elite, only to those who were ready for his universal message. He wanted, by his own admission, only pure boys to serve him. He had no time for the great moving mass of lonely souls who people this earth seeking love and forgiveness: the barflies and drug addicts, adulterers and prostitutes, tax collectors and thieves. In fact, he was too spiritually abstracted most of the time to notice much of anything.

Where, then, I asked, was his compassion? If he had any, how great could it be if he couldn't bear the touch of a needy sinner? A "savior" who is too pure to touch or be touched, I concluded, is really no savior at all, no matter how sweet his words, how deep his meditations, or how devoted his followers. To be a savior, one must be qualified—and willing—to save everyone. And only Jesus, the living testimony to God's love and mercy, displayed an eagerness to love, heal, and embrace any and all who would receive him. "Yet to all who received him, to those who believed in his name, he gave the right to become children of God" (John 1:12).

Even with this insight, however, I still hadn't fully escaped from the Eastern-Indian prisonhouse. I had wriggled free of Ramakrishna, but I remained bound by the chains of Vedanta, unable to discard my former assumptions about God, man, and creation, unable to embrace the doctrines of Christianity. In that no-man's land between Vedanta and Christianity I had only one hope—that Jesus would complete the work that he had begun in me. So I started pleading with him: "I don't know if my beliefs or actions conform to your will; so please shape my beliefs and guide my actions." Soon, eager to make the most of my new receptivity to Christ, I began to live in doubt about many of the "truths" I had formerly held to be so dear. What if, I allowed myself to ask, reincarnation *isn't* true? What if Christians *are* right and after death we go to heaven or hell, not to a new life in a new body? What if Christ really *is* the only way to the Father?

To appreciate just how radical my new receptivity was, one would have to understand the depth of my former prejudices. For over a decade I had truly believed that Christians were strange—ignorant, to be sure, but also strange. In no way could I understand them. How could any right-thinking person say, "Jesus is the only answer"? "Born again," "saved by grace through faith," "washed by the blood of the Lamb"—such catchphrases seemed comprehensible only to the spiritually immature. Christians seemed to be living not in the world that I knew but in a world that only they knew, one that was too simplistic and too rigid for thoughtful people to accept. Reincarnation, I thought, was true, period. No rational lover of God could think otherwise because no other conclusion about life and death was possible. All religions must lead to God, period. No one who is devoted to a loving God, I believed, could think otherwise.

Curiously enough, despite such prejudices, Jesus accepted me anyway—warts, doubts, and all—as I struggled to submit to him. "All right, then, even if you can't believe everything yet," he seemed to be saying, "believe in me; trust me with all your heart." And so I did, without any preconceptions about the direction my life might take. As a result I slowly slipped away from Vedanta. By April 1979 I had kicked the yoga-Vedanta habit and had stopped visiting the Vedanta Society. As though I were going through spiritual withdrawal, I began mentally to challenge and repudiate yoga-Vedantic and New-Age concepts—for example, the law of karma and the impersonal nature of deity. More importantly, I began to read Christian literature. I reflected on the conversions of Augustine, Wordsworth, T. S. Eliot, Thomas Merton, and C. S. Lewis. I tried to read as a Christian would the poetry of Dante, Donne, Bunyan, Hopkins, and T. S. Eliot. I studied the New Testament, trying to understand what its writers, as inspired by the Holy Spirit, were *really* saying. Above all, I sought, asked, and knocked, waiting for Christ's response. At last, true to his word, he responded.

Twenty-six months after I had first experienced Jesus Christ's unconditional love, I accepted him fully, unreservedly, as my Lord and Savior. With my wife and seventeen-month-old daughter, I was baptized into the Christian faith. Did I then suddenly believe everything that Christianity teaches? No. I had just decided to take the leap of faith, to empty myself, so that Jesus could fill me with his Spirit and reshape me according to his design. I had put myself in his care and joined his mystical body, the Church, for that clearly was his will.

Of course, during the past fourteen years I have had to endure many tests of my faith. The habits of a lifetime aren't easily altered, and the mind isn't renewed all at once—at least not in my case. Again and again I have haggled within myself with the old voices of Western metaphysics and yoga-Vedanta, the smug faces of my gurus hovering before my mind's eye, taunting but not daunting me. Again and again I have had to refute within myself the rationalizations of that sentimental universalism that promotes the broad way as the best and only way to God, for the words of someone like Sri Ramakrishna can be so beautifully convincing to one who loves humanity and deplores violence. We therefore shouldn't underestimate their powerful allure. For example:

> Truth is one; only It is called by different names. All people are seeking the same Truth; the variance is due to climate, temperament, and name. A lake has many ghats. From one ghat the Hindus take water in jars and call it 'jal'. From another ghat the Mussalmans take the same thing and call it 'pani'. From a third the Christians take the same thing and call it 'water'. *(All laugh.)* Suppose someone says that the thing is not 'jal' but 'pani', or that it is not 'pani' but 'water', or that it is not 'water' but 'jal'. It would be ridiculous. But this . . . is at the root of the frictions among sects. . . . This is why people injure and kill one another, and shed blood, in the name of religion. But this is not good. Everyone is going toward God. They will all realize Him if they have sincerity and longing of heart.
>
> —*M. 423*

What an irresistible message for the young idealist! "Come together," crooned the Beatles. "I'm okay, you're okay," chimed in the pop psychologists. "Yes, in every age, love is the answer," whispers the heart of the sensitive soul.

Recognizing the powerful appeal of such simple teachings, I have had to learn to trust God to give me the mind of Christ. In response, the light of Christ has made its slow advance against that old darkness. It is difficult to describe the trauma I had to endure as God slowly extricated me from the grip of Eastern philosophy. Only the hand of God can snap such mind-forged manacles. Yet even as God does so, the spiritual warfare, the clash of spiritual swords in the realm of principalities and powers, can only be barely imagined by those who have never been smitten by the exquisite beauties of Eastern mysticism. Eastern philosophy and New-Age beliefs seem so convincing precisely because they come to us cloaked in light, a light so brilliant to our benighted reason that it appears to be the light of God.

By grace, then, I have been saved, set free to enjoy an eternal relationship with Jesus Christ. And these are the only conditions I must meet: I must be true to him, for he is true to me. I must love him because he first loved me. I must remain in him because he lives in me. In Christ alone, I know, is the only real joy that I have ever known or will ever know.

Now, having shared my testimony, I shall get down to the serious business of uprooting the dead metaphysical tree of the New Age, exposing and pulverizing its twisted roots as I do so. In so doing, I can only hope that Christians might come to appreciate the extent of the deception and the formidability of the forces lined up against them. I can only pray that New-Agers of every kind might read this book with an open mind, willing to set aside their preconceptions and prejudices should they discover within these pages that the truth resides in Christ alone.

2

ONE GOD
TO FIT ALL SIZES

P ROFESSORS OF COMPARATIVE RELIGION, NEW-AGERS, AND
  yoga-Vedantins wax eloquent when they uncover the "similarities" between Christianity and other religions. They paint
their religious worldview with broad brush strokes, prone to gen-
eralize if they find the least similarity. Thus when Jesus says in
Matthew 7:13-14, "Enter through the narrow gate. For wide is
the gate and broad is the road that leads to destruction, and many
enter through it. But small is the gate and narrow the road that
leads to life, and only a few find it," a yoga-Vedantin quickly
observes that the "Katha Upanishad" says the "same" thing:

> Like the sharp edge of a razor, the sages say, is the path.
> Narrow it is, and difficult to tread.
> —*Prabhavananda, Upanishads 20*

Then, triumphal and jubilant, these prophets of the new universal generic religion of the New Age conclude that at base all
religions are one; if these "paths" seem to differ at all, they differ only in minor details over which reasonable people would
never deign to quibble.

Once they have established such "similarities," they reach for
bolder comparisons. In a book entitled *The Sermon on the
Mount According to Vedanta*, the same author above, Prab-

havananda, uniquely explicates the verse "Be perfect, therefore, as your heavenly Father is perfect" (Matt. 5:48). According to the swami—not Jesus Christ!—this perfection is the result of our realization of the God within us. Through self-effort and the attainment of purity, we discover that Brahman (the infinite, impersonal, absolute One) and Atman (the Self, or the essence of the individual soul) are one:

> When the mind has been purified through spiritual disciplines and is able to turn inward upon itself, man realizes that his true being is Atman-Brahman. To uncover this true being, or divinity, which lies hidden within oneself, is to become perfect. This is the technique of all mystical practice.
>
> —62

Notice how the mere use of the word *all* before "mystical practice" makes this yoga-Vedanta conclusion appear to be a universal truth. "Yes," the unwary student reverently whispers, "all religions are indeed one."

But the New-Age conclusion that all religions are one is a *non sequitur*. Mere similarity between a few aspects doesn't prove the identity of all aspects. In the same way that a Mack Truck and a Jaguar XKE are both vehicles and yet are very different, yoga-Vedanta and Christianity are both religions and yet are very different—in nature, form, function, and so on. Broad comparisons of this sort, like analogies, frequently break down.

Consider, for example, a famous essay written by Henry David Thoreau in which he passionately pleads for the life of John Brown, the condemned leader of the revolt at Harper's Ferry. Hoping to glorify Brown by associating him with an indisputably innocent man, he likens Brown to Jesus Christ. If we closely examine Thoreau's analogy, however, it quickly falls apart. True, Jesus was considered radical by the authorities of his day, and he did have only a few zealous disciples. But he never took up arms in defense of his cause, and he never murdered anyone as John Brown had. None of the gospels portray a wild-eyed Jesus holed up in the Temple, chucking spears at a Roman legion.

When comparisons between like items are multiplied, they may impress us, and yet they still prove nothing. A clever counterfeiter can produce a convincing semblance of an original Rembrandt. But the counterfeited Rembrandt can never become the original. The discerning art lover and the savvy collector will know the difference.

Nevertheless, exactly in this way New-Age teachers constantly appeal to such "similarities" between Christianity and other religions. They then promote a vision of world-wide religious unity. Yet, in so doing, they indirectly—and sometimes directly—undermine the uniqueness and authority of Christianity. Doctrine and dogma—so runs their argument—are divisive. In this modern world, only the unenlightened cling to them. The real spiritual seekers, perceiving the similarities between religions, eschew dogma and advocate universal toleration and harmony. Finding God within themselves, they respect all paths and yet trod the unique path that God outlines for them. God is one; the truth is one. "*Ekam sat vipra bahudda vadanti,*" they sing in harmony with the ancient seers of India: "As many faiths, so many paths." And it makes so much sense to them that no other explanation can make any sense.

But how do these New-Age seekers arrive at such conclusions? All such conclusions are based, first and foremost, on a faulty conception of God, a conception that has its roots in the yoga-Vedanta philosophy—namely, in the soil of India. As the oldest, most sophisticated natural religion in the world, yoga-Vedanta lends credence to almost any New-Age conception of God. *Satchitananda*, God as absolute existence (*sat*), consciousness (*chit*), and bliss (*ananda*) becomes life, light, and love or Cosmic Consciousness; *Atman*, the Self, becomes the True Self, Christ Self, or Higher Self; *shakti*, the imminent, creative energy of God, becomes the Higher Power. Against this ancient theological backdrop, New-Agers authoritatively—and often offhandedly—use such time-honored Sanskrit terms as *karma*, *guru*, *maya*, and *samadhi*, thereby trying to silence all debate. Shushed by ancient, mysterious gobbledygook, would-be disciples are then supposed to submit to the authority of these "universal truths" and accept the mysteries of their newfound faith.

Because yoga-Vedanta provides the chief philosophical underpinning of New-Age thinking, its theology must necessarily be understood if New-Age theology as a whole is to be understood. Therefore, in this chapter and the ones that follow, we will be examining the New-Age Movement's fundamental *a priori* assumptions about God, nature, and man in light of the formulations of yoga-Vedanta.

THE EAST-WEST THEOLOGICAL CONNECTION

God the Transcendent

As a rule, the most orthodox yoga-Vedantins are strict monists (or non-dualists). That is, they believe that God *alone* exists. God is One without a second. "Brahman alone is—nothing else is. He who sees the manifold universe, and not the one reality, goes evermore from death to death" (*Upanishads* 21). Seen in this light, God is impersonal and transcendent: "[It] is birthless and deathless. It neither grows nor decays. It is unchangeable, eternal" (Shankara, *Crest Jewel* 53). As such "It" is beyond the reach of mind and speech: "Brahman is the reality—the one existence, absolutely independent of human thought and idea" (Shankara, *Crest Jewel* 67).

To make this stark God comprehensible, the monists liken It to an infinite, omnipresent ocean of light. Waves rise and fall on its surface, but Brahman always remains whole, unchanged. The waves have no absolute existence, precisely because they are transitory extensions of Brahman, mere phenomena. Whether the waves rise or fall, they are always comprised of the same substance: Brahman. In fact, to the wise, the waves—space-time, matter, and energy, including all creatures and objects, natural or supernatural—are Brahman. Hence, Brahman alone exists. Using this same metaphor, the monists claim that you and I, as individual souls, are like glass jars on the floor of the ocean. Each jar is filled with and immersed in Brahman at all times. When a jar is broken—that is, when one's sense of "I" is destroyed through the practice of yoga—all that remains is the ocean, which, as always, is absolute, infinite, changeless, pure, eternal, incomprehensible to the mind. Upon the attainment of that state of oneness, an individual overcomes sorrow, evil, and death:

> He who knows Brahman becomes Brahman. No one ignorant is ever born in his family. He passes beyond all sorrow. He overcomes evil. Freed from the fetters of ignorance he becomes immortal.
>
> —*Upanishads 48*

From this point on, according to the monists, the liberated soul—forever aware of his true nature—experiences endless bliss.

God the Imminent

Such heights, however, are difficult for the average mind to scale. Most spiritual seekers, so say the yoga-Vedantins, can't remain for long in the rarefied atmosphere of *advaita*, the monistic school of yoga-Vedanta. For this reason, the seers who wrote the various upanishads included verses for less austere—namely, "less evolved"—souls also, those who can't help feeling that the created universe is real. Thus, within yoga-Vedanta another school has arisen to accommodate these seekers: qualified monism (*vashistadvaita*). Instead of declaring that Brahman is the only reality, this school argues that Brahman is one thing and the individual soul another.

Once again using metaphors, the qualified monists explain the relationship in this way: Brahman is like the sun; the individual souls are like its rays. Or again, Brahman is like a pomegranate; individual souls are like its seeds. According to Ramanuja, the chief exponent of this theology, Brahman and individual souls are one but distinct and separable. As one scholar puts it:

> God, though he has transformed himself into the universe of sentient and nonsentient forms, remains distinct from them. Matter is the object of experience, individual souls are the experiencing subjects, and God is the lord and ruler of all. He is defined in the Upanishads . . . as . . . real . . . conscious . . . and infinite. Ramanuja . . . points out that because of these distinctive attributes God is above and beyond matter (which is changing phenomena) and distinct from individual souls caught in its meshes. Thus, though the universe is a transformation of Brahman, he remains by his nature beyond change, and though imminent, he is transcendent.
> —*Prabhavananda, The Spiritual Heritage 309*

In this way, the qualified monists can have it both ways. They can worship a personal, imminent God and at the same time affirm that he is transcendent.

In fact, there are many passages in *The Upanishads* themselves that can be interpreted as either monistic, qualified monistic, or both. Consider the following passage from the "Svetasvatara Upanishad":

> The one absolute, impersonal Existence, together with his inscrutable Maya [power of illusion], appears as the divine Lord, the personal God, endowed with manifold glories. By his divine power he holds dominion over all the worlds. At the periods of creation and dissolution of the universe, he alone exists. Those who realize him become immortal.

The Lord is One without a second. Within man he dwells, and within all other beings. He projects the universe, maintains it, and withdraws it into himself.

His eyes are everywhere; his face, his arms, his feet are in every place. Out of himself he has produced the heavens and the earth, and with his arms and his wings he holds them together.

—Upanishads 121-22

Here God is "the divine Lord, the personal God, endowed with manifold glories" and also "One without a second." At certain times "he alone exists"; at other times "He projects the universe."

And the statement "Out of himself he has produced the heavens and the earth" actually cuts both ways. Both monists and qualified monists—indeed, all yoga-Vedantins—believe that God is both the efficient and material cause of the universe. As the First and Only Cause, "he fills the universe" and "transcends it" (*Upanishads* 122). As such, he is pure existence and consciousness: "He is the one light that gives light to all. He shining, everything shines" (*Upanishads* 23). At the same time, however, "As threads come out of the spider, as little sparks come out of the fire, so all the senses, all the worlds, all the gods, yea, all beings" issue forth from him (*Upanishads* 86). Another verse defines this relationship between Brahman and his creation even more precisely:

Brahman willed that it should be so, and brought forth out of himself the material cause of the universe; from this came the primal energy, and from the primal energy mind, from mind the subtle elements, from the subtle elements the many worlds, and from the acts performed by beings in the many worlds the chain of cause and effect [the law of karma]—the reward and punishment of works.

—Upanishads 43-44

Therefore, to the yoga-Vedantin, everything in creation—you, I, a tree, a mosquito, a cow patty—is comprised of God's own substance. Whether the monists say that creation is an illusion superimposed by us in our ignorance upon the One or the qualified monists say that creation is real, God and his creation are fundamentally the same. Clearly, despite the protestations of many intellectual yoga-Vedantins, their theology remains unabashedly pantheistic. If all that exists is made of God's substance, then God is a substance; if God is a substance, then all that exists must be, in some sense, God.

God the True Self

Although, as you shall soon see, *Self* is a favorite buzzword among Western occultists and New-Age thinkers, the concept of the True Self (Atman) has its roots in yoga-Vedanta. In *The Upanishads*, *The Bhagavad Gita*, and most of the modern yoga handbooks as well, the attainment of the True Self is said to be the supreme goal of every man and woman. Through spiritual disciplines and meditation on the True Self, a person becomes God:

> Ridding the mind of all impurities and fixing it on Atman—these are the twofold intents on which the [spiritual seeker] engages himself. The mind becomes all-powerful as it gains in purity. Because of its purity it gains access to Atman. The greatest and the holiest of its achievements lies in its getting fixed in the Atman. Man becomes god through this benign act of the mind.
> —*Chidbhavananda 758*

To the follower of qualified monism, when the spiritual seeker discovers his True Self, he realizes that he is a piece of God, a spark of that Infinite Fire—namely, Brahman. In acknowledgment of this distinction between the Atman (the Self) and

Brahman (God), the above passage says, "Man becomes god," with a lower case *g*, implying that an illumined man becomes "God-like" but not God the Absolute. But as shown earlier, the strict monists make no such distinction:

> Self-realization and God-realization are not two different experiences. In realizing the self we realize God. In realizing God we realize the self. The self and God are subjective and objective views of the same Reality. . . . In the relative plane it is the Eternal Subject, the Soul of all souls. The direct approach to It is, therefore, through the self. This is why we seek God with closed eyes in the inmost depth of our being.
>
> *—Satprakashananda 24*

Hence, Atman equals Brahman—the Self equals God. "*Aham Brahmasmi*"—"I am Brahman"—declares one upanishad; "*Tat tvam asi*"—"Thou art That"—declares another. The path to Brahman, we are told, is an inward one, a passage through the self, an entirely subjective search for that which already exists within each person as his True Self—namely, Brahman, the Godhead.

The New-Age Movement—Western Occultism, New Thought, Theosophy, Unity, Religious Science, and the like—appears to derive its sense of the self from a basic yoga-Vedantic premise: "In the heart of all things, of whatever there is in the universe, dwells the Lord" (*Upanishads* 27). Thus, according to New-Agers the inner self of every human being is divine. They further rationalize this conception of the self as divine by quoting Christ: "The kingdom of heaven is within you" and "I and my Father are one." These words, so the argument runs, prove that the "Christ Self" resides in each of us and that this "Christ Self," to the illumined soul, is identical with God, at least in the sense that it possesses, *in toto*, God's knowledge, power, and love. Using the term "Secret Self," one writer puts it this way:

To fully uncover the Secret Self is no doubt the final goal of evolution. When the inhabiting spirit has fully emerged from matter, then the Godhead will be revealed at last with all its conscious power and infinite realization.

—*Anderson, Magic 46*

With the use of the passive voice here, however—"the Godhead will be revealed"—the writer doesn't actually say that God and the Self are one. He merely implies it. For a bolder assertion that identifies man with God, we need to turn to the words of an occultist:

My consciousness and your consciousness are God's Consciousness! We are the Creative Spirit in Its aspect of both the One and the Many. Your flesh and my flesh are forms that the Self takes. . . . Your body is a Temple for the Living God!

—*Davies 22*

Despite the apparent agreement between Western New-Age teachers and the Eastern gurus, the Western New-Age "theologians" are rarely consistent, for they have never devised a coherent theology as the yoga-Vedantins have. By comparison they are sloppy thinkers. In the same publication quoted above, the writer claims with equal fervor: "We are part and parcel of the limitless Absolute Consciousness" (Davies 4). Previously she asserted that we are identified with God's consciousness; now she asserts that we are merely part of it. Are we, then, all of It or just part of It? In what sense can we be aspects "of both the One and the Many"? Only one who in fact hates reason and enlightenment can speak in such terms, for it would be difficult for a rational person to argue that the part—say, a kneecap—is the whole— namely, a human body; or that the one—a human—is the many—namely, three billion people.

Most New-Agers draw from many sources—Cabalism,

Hermeticism, yoga-Vedanta, Gnosticism, Pythagoreanism, even Christianity. This eclecticism, this desire for the esoteric and arcane, may account for their confusion. They spin up and down the ages, from culture to culture in their quest for "Knowledge" and, most especially, "Experiences." One moment they turn to astrology, then to tarot, then to Theosophy, then to hatha yoga, and then to spiritism. The next moment, they may subscribe to crystal power, wear amulets, worship the goddess, engage in past-life readings, or scan the skies for UFOs. They are, therefore, not really concerned about logic or consistency. Basically, if it feels good, they believe it or do it.

This illogic takes many forms. Consider this definition of the Higher Self from a manuscript I was asked to edit many years ago, a book written by a man with a Ph.D. from a respected English university and an M.A. from an accredited American state college:

> The Higher SELF is represented by your soul and spirit. The soul is comprised of two parts, your Higher SELF and the Godhead. The personality of these two aspects of your soul is your spirit. The spirit is Christ in you, the enlightened part of you.

Regardless of the man's credentials, we have a right to ask for clarification. How can the Higher SELF be equal to the soul, for example, and then be only one aspect of—or one half of—the soul? In what sense does he mean "personality"? And how can these "two aspects" be said to have a personality? Finally, how is the "Christ in you, the enlightened part in you" related to the "Higher SELF"? Analyze it. Like many New-Age formulations, it's all a muddle.

Still, if we were to align New-Agers with a particular theological worldview, we would discover that most of them camp among the qualified monists. Edgar Cayce, one of the most revered gurus of the movement, states this view quite simply, if

not quite as poetically as the yoga-Vedantins: "For ye are as a cor-
puscle in the body of God; thus a co-creator with Him"
(Gammon 13). New-Agers may often wax eloquent about the
Higher Self, but they almost always return to qualified monism,
and for good reason. They want to remain separate from God,
not because they are devotees intent on worshiping God as the
yoga-Vedantins seem to be, but because they literally want to be
co-creators with God. They want, above all else, occult power,
success, fame, wealth—in short, the good life. By remaining separate from God, they can follow and fulfill their own desires and
disregard the commandments of God.

God the Limitless, All-powerful Mind-Substance

Most New-Agers don't identify with the ancient seers of *The
Upanishads* who sat cross-legged in loincloths beneath tamarind
trees contemplating the truth. Instead, they are more likely to
identify with Shirley MacLaine, L. Ron Hubbard, or Anthony
Robbins. They are more likely to want new clothes or cars, personal magnetism, psychic abilities, perfect health, or simple peace
of mind. As a rule, then, they leave the theologizing to someone
else. They want results.

To feed this hunger for results, New-Age teachers exhort their
followers to look within themselves, into their subconscious
minds, and find the "Secret of the ages," the "Infinite Power
within," their "Limitless Supply." If they will only draw upon this
"Limitless Substance" within, they will be able to have, do, or be
whatever they desire: "Think and feel exhaustless riches in relationships and material requirements, and then draw it from the
All! You are wealthy beyond comprehension!" (Davies 11). And
how do they "tap into" this power? They must merely affirm the
"truth":

> It is the Father's good pleasure to give me the kingdom of
> unlimited supply, and it is my good pleasure to receive it. I

am receiving. I am receiving all the wealth God has for me,
and God has unlimited wealth for me now!
—*Ponder, Open Your Mind 174*

God, it seems, wants everyone to have "unlimited wealth," even
in a finite world with limited resources. The kingdom of God, it
seems, is a substance within us and around us, just waiting to be
tapped.

"The All [God] is mind," these teachers further tell us, drawing upon the conclusion of the Hermeticists, the disciples of the
so-called ancient Egyptian teacher Hermes (Three Initiates 26).
As here defined, God is both an Infinite Mind and an
omnipresent creative substance. Because everything in the universe is mental, vibrating with energy, we can draw upon this
Limitless, Omnipotent Mind-Substance at will and shape our
own lives as we wish:

> The whole teaching of the *Bhagavad Gita* which has been
> the inspiration of uncounted millions through centuries, is
> that there is but one Reality and that this Reality is to us
> what we believe it to be. Everything comes from one
> Substance, or Reality, and our thought qualifies and condi-
> tions that Substance and determines what is to take place in
> our lives.
> —*Williams 186*

Thus God, as Limitless Mind-Substance, is there for the taking.
He is there to do our bidding, like a genie, or a charge card with
an unlimited line of credit, or an electric outlet. And to the extent
that we "open" ourselves to him, we become co-creators with
him. We become fully aware corpuscles "in the body of God,"
creating for ourselves whatever we want.

Does this approach sound too good to be true? Well, of
course, it does, because it is. When a teacher who is proffering
such teachings comes to you, you had better hide your money

under your mattress. In his attempt to help you "feel good" for a few days or weeks, he will most likely "prosper" himself at your expense and use you as another success story for his next best-selling book to boot. Soon enough afterwards, when real life grabs you by the throat and squeezes the PMA (positive mental attitude) out of you, you will find little consolation in his books and tapes or in that autographed glossy photograph of his beaming face that you received "free" at his seminar.

THE ERRORS IN THIS THEOLOGY

All of these conceptions of God, from the blatantly materialistic to the monistic, are false, for four important reasons.

God Isn't a Substance

As Thomas Aquinas asserted centuries ago in his *Summa Theologica* (Question III, Article 7), a substance found among other substances must be part of a compound. Simply put, when we pour a bag of powdered Koolaid and two cups of sugar into a pitcher of water, the result is a compound: a sweet, fruity drink. Two substances have been mixed with a third to form a new compound.

In the same way, if God were a substance that may be found in our subconsciousness or consciousness, that is, within our mortal frame, then as a substance it must necessarily mingle with our mortal substances, with flesh, bones, brain tissue, neurons, biochemicals, molecules, and so on. A God such as this would therefore be part of a compound—a mind-body-god compound. Clearly, however, this God-Substance that is said to indwell and permeate us can't be God, because every compound changes. And God, who is immaterial and uncompounded, doesn't change. If he does, he isn't God. Therefore, the New-Agers' god isn't God but something else—at best, a natural energy; at worst, an attractive but dangerous monster.

Furthermore, as Augustine informed us in his *Confessions*

(Book VII.I.2), if God were a substance, he would be present to a greater or lesser degree in creatures according to their size. Big Bertha, the circus elephant, would then have more "god" in her than would, say, Mother Theresa. Conceivably such large crea-tures—consider dinosaurs also—would be holier and wiser than humans based solely on their bulk rather than their brain power. He who possessed more of the God-Substance would be more godly. Clearly this conclusion is absurd.

For these same reasons, New-Agers can't assert that God is the *material* cause of the universe. Saying so would once again be affirming that God is a transitory substance that assumes numberless forms, from a supernova to a firefly, from a mass murderer to an AIDS virus. "But," such people argue, "God doesn't create *ex nihilo* (out of nothing). Instead, he pulls the sub-stance of creation out of himself." Yet if the God-Substance that comes out of an eternal God is transitory and impermanent when it takes the form of the universe, doesn't that make God himself transitory and impermanent by nature? Unless we are willing to be inconsistent and illogical, we can't declare that any material substance, however fine, ever existed in or as God, the absolutely changeless and eternal.

Therefore, God can't be a substance. He can't be, for that rea-son, an energy, a vibration, or even "spiritual stuff," for all of these may be mixed with other substances, intermingled with them, to form new compounds and variations.

God Is That Than Which Nothing Greater Can Be Conceived

As shown above, God can't be a substance because substances change. But we can also argue that God can't be a physical, men-tal, or spiritual substance because we can easily conceive of a God who is greater than any kind of substance, however fine we may conceive that substance to be. Greater than any substance is spirit—in particular, formless, substanceless, pure, infinite, eternal, omnipresent, all-wise, all-powerful, all-good Spirit. Beyond such a conception the mind can't go. Beyond it lies an infinitude of silence, in the face of which we can only whisper, "He is" and kneel before his own self-description: "I AM that I AM."

Therefore, when Western occultists speak of the "All-Mind" or "Mind-Substance" or "the Power within," they aren't speaking of God. They are referring to something natural rather than supernatural, finite rather than infinite, transitory rather than eternal. Even if they protest, saying, "No, that's not what we mean—we are talking about substances and powers that belong to God," they have still landed in a minefield. How, we might ask, can we falsely claim and manipulate, according to our own purposes, those substances and powers that belong to God without regard to his will—indeed, without worshiping him as he is?

God Is Sovereign

A God who is merely a substance or power that you or I can draw upon at will to do, be, or have anything we want isn't the Sovereign, unless we were to argue that the Sovereign permits us to be sovereign, in which case there could be no sole Sovereign. But if such were possible, each of us, if we were adept enough at manipulating the Mind-Substance, would be able to fulfill all our desires. Obviously, however, such creative autonomy is impossible because my desires must at times conflict with yours. If two sovereign beings want the same job, only one can obtain it. Who, then, knows what is best for the two people—or sovereign wills—that are involved? Only a sovereign God, who knows what each of us deserves and needs. Therefore, although God may possess power, he cannot be employed according to our wills. Otherwise, he wouldn't be God, the Sovereign.

Moreover, the Sovereign, being omniscient, must necessarily know things that you or I can't know because our finite minds aren't omniscient. God transcends the mind. He is, for this reason, greater even than the sum of all our minds. Clearly, as contingent, finite, mortal beings we aren't wise enough to be the Sovereign. If we think we are, we are making the same mistake Adam and Eve made in the Garden when they listened to the insinuations of the serpent and chose self-assertion over obedience. We do, to be sure, have free wills, but we aren't free to "use" God's will as we wish. If we could, we would have no need of a God. Others would be right to call us atheists.

God and His Creation Are Absolutely Real

Now we come to the last, most difficult, most fundamental problem posed by the strict monists. If, as the monists insist, creation isn't real in the absolute sense, then we can't infer the existence of a real Creator from our observation of phenomena. If creation is an illusion, we can only at best say that creation may or may not be. For this reason we would have to remain agnostics, for we could only at best also say that God may or may not be. How could we infer a First Cause from a creation that either may or may not exist? Our common sense—our belief that we live in a real and orderly universe—would then be ignorance. And Paul, speaking as one inspired by God, would be a liar: "For since the creation of the world God's invisible qualities—his eternal power and divine nature—have been clearly seen, being understood from what has been made, so that men are without excuse" (Rom. 1:20). Therefore, precisely because creation *is* indeed real, we may infer that God is the Creator of that creation.

To avoid such objections, the monistic yoga-Vedantins tell us that all descriptions of God are maya—mere illusory superimpositions on the Only Reality, Brahman. Everything short of Brahman is relative. Thus we must experience Brahman directly to understand Brahman. In this way they avoid the intellectual problems by simply saying that God can't be defined or clarified by means of language. Only direct experience of Brahman, they claim, can reveal him as he is, at which point the illumined sage just *knows*. With one sweep of the hand, then, they dismiss any attempts to challenge the logic or truthfulness of their assertions. In short, they beg the question.

This smug appeal to "experience" may signal the end of the discussion but not of the practical problems. Now we slip into the icy and unpredictable waters of subjectivism, where there is no objective truth and where every man is, ultimately, his own authority. Were this really the only way by which we could arrive at the Truth, God would be most cruelly stranding us in those deadly, indifferent waters. We wouldn't be permitted to use reason save in the form of paradoxes and negations (God is not this, not that); nor would we be given any revelations by God to direct us, since God isn't *really* a creator and therefore isn't *really* personally involved in or concerned about creation—or the creatures, like you and me, who have to make their way through often bewildering circumstances and dilemmas.

With what, then, are we left to guide and illumine us? With subjective experiences, in particular the experiences of the "illumined" seers—remote in the form of the *Shruti* (the *Upanishads*, *The Bhagavad Gita*), immediate in the form of gurus (modern-day avatars, masters, and swamis) and, even worse, channelers and all their ilk. Ultimately, for the spiritual seeker it's simply an intuitively grasped "feeling" that determines his choice of guru and hence his choice of authority and practice.

And here, as we shall find again and again in the next several chapters, yoga-Vedanta and Western Occultism meet theologically—in the icy, treacherous waters of subjectivism. Here they merge, and we are left with the New-Age Movement, a heterodox hodgepodge that welcomes diversity and inconsistencies, celebrates subjective intuitions and "experiences," and exalts Self above all objective authority. To such people, objectively revealed truth is relative, subjectively revealed truth absolute.

3

THE UNIVERSE: WHEELS WITHIN WHEELS

WHY ARE YOU IN SUCH A HURRY?" MY GURU ONCE asked me with a chuckle when I was complaining to him, with great anguish, that I kept forgetting God amid the hubbub of my daily work. "Do you think you will go to hell?" At the time his question had its intended effect. It snapped me back to "reality." Of course not, I thought. As a yoga-Vedantin I knew that I had many lives ahead of me, as many as I needed. There was no reason to be anxious. If I couldn't realize God in this life, then I would realize him in the next, or the one after that. I knew, as my fellow yoga-Vedantins knew, that I probably had much karma to "burn off" before I could attain God-consciousness, achieving liberation from the rounds of birth and death.

Like all the other deluded people in the world, I was caught, I realized, in the meshes of maya, illusion. I was trapped in *samsara*, the endless cycle of births and deaths, because I erroneously believed not only that I was one thing and Brahman was another, but also that the universe was one thing and Brahman was another. Until I realized that Brahman alone is real, the Law would have me by the throat and exact its price. According to my deeds in this life and my former lives, it would sometimes reward me, sometimes punish me. But always I would be bound to the wheel until I became a fully conscious, liberated "knower of God."

Because of the yoga-Vedantic assumptions about the nature of God, many people, as I did, readily adopt the Eastern view of the universe. If God is the efficient *and* material cause of creation, then he must *be* creation—or at least what we think is creation. Yet if that is the case, why are we ignorant of the Truth, and what can we do about our ignorance if we wish to be "masters" of ourselves and our circumstances? Yoga-Vedantins and New-Agers offer remarkably similar answers.

THE NEW-AGE CONCEPTION OF THE UNIVERSE

It stands to reason that if a basic premise is false, then the conclusion, whether reached validly or not, will be false too. Such is the case with the New-Age conception of the universe. Once God is viewed as an impersonal material cause, then the universe he has created will also be falsely defined and interpreted. Whether the New-Age theologians buttress their view by blaming our bondage on maya, *prakriti* (a term I will explain shortly), karma, or all three, they launch us down a dangerous, tortuous path that leads us farther and farther away from the truth.

Maya

Although the concept of maya is mostly confined to Hinduism, it's nevertheless foundational to our understanding of the New-Age cosmology, for it reveals the source of a recurrent theme in all New-Age materials: all limitations are illusory. In short, the fact that you or I *seem* to be limited creatures, limited in potential, willpower, and action, is an illusion. Dr. Ann Davies, like other New-Age theologians, thunders this message over and over again: "What can limit the power of our consciousness? Only the false belief in limitation" (10). And so does Charles Fillmore, the founder of the Unity School of Christianity:

No person or thing in the universe, no chain of circumstances, can by any possibility interpose itself between you
and all joy—all good. You may think that something stands
between you and your heart's desire, and so live with that
desire unfulfilled, but it is not true. . . . Deny it, and you will
find yourself free. . . . Then you will see the good flowing to
you, and you will see that nothing can stand between you
and your own.

—*Ponder, Open Your Mind 19*

Thus, if we can deny a limitation and, in doing so, find ourselves
free, the limitation must have always been an illusion. It was
never true in the first place.

For the origin of the concept of maya, however, we must turn
to Shankara, the eighth-century East-Indian monist, because he
precisely defined and popularized the term. According to him, the
phenomenal universe, consisting of matter and thought, isn't real.
Even so, paradoxically it does exist. Therefore, it is and isn't at
the same time:

Here, then, we are confronted with a paradox—the world is
and is not. It is neither real nor unreal. And yet this apparent
paradox is a statement of fact—a fact which Shankara calls
Maya. This Maya, this world-appearance, has its basis in
Brahman, the eternal. The concept of Maya applies only to
the phenomenal world, which . . . consists of names and
forms. It is not non-existent, yet it differs from . . . Brahman,
upon which it depends for its existence. It is not real, since it
disappears in the light of knowledge of its eternal basis.
World-appearance is Maya; the Self, the Atman, alone is real.

—*Shankara, Crest-Jewel, Introduction 15-16*

Despite Shankara's philosophical paradox—his attempt to
explain our very real experience of the phenomenal universe—
most popularizers of the concept don't make such subtle distinc-

tions. A recent "avatar," Sri Ramakrishna, has put it more simply. Before one realizes God, "This world is . . . a 'framework of illusion', unreal as a dream." But after one realizes God, he "finds that [God] alone has become maya, the universe, and all living beings" (M., 836). Apparently illumination transforms the seeker into a pantheist for whom everything becomes God.

According to such monists, we are bound by maya because we are ignorant of our true nature. For some mysterious reason, we superimpose the universe upon Brahman. Like a man on a footpath at dusk who mistakes a rope for a snake, we falsely regard the universe to be real. As a result, we become subject to the dualities of life: attraction and repulsion, pleasure and pain, love and hate, joy and sorrow. We then find ourselves revolving on the wheel of *samsara*, attached to the unreal. Thus bound, we eventually begin to feel limited, unfulfilled, empty, alienated from God. Only by becoming disillusioned by the dualities of life and then by desiring freedom from the endless rounds of births and deaths can we begin to escape from maya.

At this point, we find ourselves prepared to deny the existence of maya, saying, "*neti, neti*"—"not this, not this." Brahman isn't this, nor is he that. By negation and denial we find that he isn't the universe, nor is he any God that we can imagine. Nor is he nature, other people, the body, the mind, thoughts, desires, feelings, the ego, and so on. Having begun this process of stripping away the veils of ignorance that cover the Truth, we eventually, the monists argue, arrive at the knowledge that all is Brahman, the Unlimited One without a second:

> The universe no longer exists after we have awakened into the highest consciousness in the eternal Atman, which is Brahman, devoid of any distinction or division. At no time— either past, present, or future—is there really a snake within the rope or a drop of water in the mirage.
>
> —*Shankara, Crest-Jewel 92-93*

And this awakened state the yoga-Vedantins call *mukti*, liberation. In it no limitations exist because no limitations ever did exist. The seeker then can declare, "*Aham Brahmasmi*" ("I am Brahman").

Prakriti

Obviously Shankara's state of and approach to liberation are too austere for most Western seekers. When they strip away the veils of ignorance, they want to find the good life, not Brahman. They want to master themselves and their circumstances. They would prefer to follow *A Course in Miracles*, a book much touted today in New-Age circles, and learn how to attract to themselves—or bring into manifestation in their lives—health, success, and wealth. They want to think positively and control their minds so that they can live more abundantly. Some may even want to become "masters."

Yet here, with the word *master* (used both as a noun and a verb), Eastern and Western seekers meet, for they all believe that the power of God resides in nature—both as mind and matter— as a kind of elemental, undifferentiated, malleable substance or energy (Prabhavananda and Isherwood, *How to Know God* 25ff.). This primal substance the yoga-Vedantins call *prakriti*. It's the real stuff of which everything is made—from a supernova to a quark. It's the material that Brahman projects from himself at the beginning of an age and withdraws into himself at the close of an age. It's *Mahat*, the Great Cause from which the universe evolves, from the subtlest essences (thought waves, gamma waves, and so on) to the grossest material objects (rocks and stones and trees).

Thus New-Agers of every kind can declare, "In truth, the whole universe is God in manifestation." "The one cause, the eternal unit," claims Manly P. Hall, "is diversified into the millions of existing forms, all of which bear witness to the infinite diversity of powers concealed within the structure of the primitive One" (*Collected Writings*, III 65). In its feminine aspect, it's nature; in its masculine aspect, it's the impersonal, vitalizing One: "[Nature] is the negative pole of life, called by ancients the Divine Mother, in contrast to the vitalizing ray which carries the title of Great Father" (*Collected Writings*, III 68-69). Apparently borrowing from the Hindus, who worship *Shakti*, the feminine or negative principle, and *Shiva*, the masculine or positive principle, Western occultists will thus often refer to their "Mother-Father God" who orders, pervades, and comprises all things.

In this way New-Agers worship both nature and God, regarding natural things as symbols for God: "He who sees all forms as symbols of reality is well on the way to touching the unveiled Self" (Bailey 76). Just as the Hindus worship the many forms of the Divine Mother—*Durga, Lakshmi, Prajapati, Kali*—New-Agers turn with equal zeal to their "symbols" of God—idols, stars and planets, tarot shapes and colors, numerals, geometrical figures, and so on. Consider, for example, the symbol of the serpent. In Western Occultism it signifies wisdom, especially when the serpent is depicted as forming a circle and biting its own tail. In Eastern mysticism, especially *Tantric* yoga, it signifies the coiled power of God that resides at the base of the spine, called the *kundalini*. Because of this common symbol, New-Agers glibly adopt the term *kundalini* and talk about the seven centers in the body (using the term "third eye," for example, instead of the Sanskrit word *ajna*), which must be stimulated or awakened as the *kundalini* begins to rise by means of psychic disciplines.

Finally, by learning how to control and direct such powers of *prakriti*, New-Agers and yoga-Vedantins alike gain *siddhis*, "psychic powers." The yoga-Vedantins, who feel that *siddhis* can enhance one's spiritual progress, acquire their *siddhis* by withdrawing their senses into themselves (as a tortoise withdraws its limbs) and by concentrating on pure existence, consciousness, and bliss. The New-Agers acquire their "psychic powers" by thinking positively and denying the existence of limitations, drawing their power from the subconscious, "the infinite storehouse within." In both cases a person "expands his consciousness" by adopting some systematic routine or method and vigorously practicing it. In the end, the result is the same: yoga-Vedantins and New-Agers both are to become "masters" of themselves and, in some sense, also of their circumstances. They are to use *prakriti* and the laws of the universe to effect their release from ignorance and bondage.

Karma

The chief of all the laws is the law of karma, sometimes called the law of cause and effect. On this point New-Agers and yoga-Vedantins fully agree: the inexorable law of karma governs the universe on a cosmic and microcosmic scale, on the spiritual and human planes. According to Western tradition, the concept may be traced to the *Kybalion* of Hermes Trismegistus:

> Every Cause has its Effect; every Effect has its Cause; everything happens according to Law; Chance is but a name for Law not recognized; there are many planes of causation, but nothing escapes the Law.

> —*Three Initiates 171*

But in the West today, it's the Eastern conception that is most popularly accepted. In a general sense, karma refers to "volitional action" (Satprakashananda 130). More specifically, however, karma takes three different forms. First, it may take the form of *sanchita karma*, the impressions left by the sum total of all our actions, good and bad, since the beginning of our existence, past lives included. Then there is *prarabdha karma*, only that portion of karma drawn from the storehouse of sanchita karma that we are reaping in our present lives. Finally, there is *kriyamana karma,* the karma that we are now in the process of sowing, for good or ill, according to the way we use our free wills (Shivananda 186-87).

Other authorities also distinguish between good karma, *shubha karma;* bad karma, *ashubha karma;* and the fruits of karma, *karma-phala* (Nirvedananda 38-39). In both the East and West, of course, this law can only work if every human being lives a multitude of lives, for otherwise yoga-Vedantins and New-Agers can't explain why a child may be born with Down's syndrome or why a serial killer may go unpunished during his lifetime. The theory of reincarnation itself, however, will be discussed in a later chapter.

To grasp this theory of karma, let's consider two popular sayings to which New-Agers often appeal in support of their concept of karma.

As you sow, so shall you reap. As Christians will recognize, these words represent a paraphrase of Paul's words, "Do not be deceived: God cannot be mocked. A man reaps what he sows" (Gal. 6:7). True to form, New-Agers quote the Bible whenever it suits their occultic or universalistic purposes, even if they quote a passage out of context, as they do here. Thus they themselves are guilty of "proof-texting" or what they themselves might disdainfully call "Bible-thumping," not only because they fail to consider the theme of the Epistle to the Galatians as a whole, but also because they fail to include the next three most telling verses:

> *The one who sows to please his sinful nature, from that nature will reap destruction; the one who sows to please the Spirit, from the Spirit will reap eternal life. Let us not become weary in doing good, for at the proper time we will reap a harvest if we do not give up. Therefore, as we have opportunity, let us do good to all people, especially to those who belong to the family of believers.*

The sowing and reaping to which Paul refers seems to be of an ultimate kind. It leads people either to death or eternal life, not to wealth or poverty, health or sickness, according to their karma. In fact, if we Christians live by the Spirit, who knows what we need better than we do, we will not gratify the desires of the sinful nature (5:16-18). Paul assures us, on the other hand, that those who follow their sinful nature won't inherit the kingdom of God (5:19-21). They will "reap destruction." We Christians are therefore instructed to continue in "doing good," living by the Spirit and producing the fruit of the Holy Spirit (5:22-25), not so we might obtain material rewards—which indeed may never be ours—but that we might reap the ultimate spiritual "harvest"—eternal life in Christ Jesus. With just a hint of a warning aimed at Christians, Paul urges us not to lose heart even if the fruit of our obedience, heaven, seems far off, but to continue to do good to all people, especially believers.

Therefore, the sowing and reaping to which Paul refers has absolutely nothing to do with manipulating karma, using mind power, or thinking our way to wealth and health. As Paul has made so abundantly clear elsewhere in his letters, we are saved not by works, but by grace through faith.

Even given this analysis, New-Agers continue to resist the Christian understanding of this passage, for one simple reason: they are prejudiced against orthodox Christianity. This is why they will neither strive to understand Pauline theology in its entirety, nor consider it in its larger context—the Bible as a whole. If they did, they might have to confront a great many biblical positions with which they disagree: the real existence of an eternal heaven and hell, Christ's unique claim to sonship, and so on. In point of fact, however, they lack the intellectual integrity to examine all the evidence. They would rather pick and choose among those passages that appear to support their preconceptions.

As for the rest of the Bible, they will leave it to us "unevolved" spiritual thinkers who are too myopic to see past the "literal interpretations," unaware that biblical exegesis is far more sophisticated than they have ever imagined. It's easier for them to turn us Christians into straw men and women who lack the brains to interpret Scripture rightly than to explore the matter in depth.

So the New-Agers plunge ahead, explaining that Paul's words prove that there is indeed a law of karma, even if Christians are unwilling to acknowledge it. Every good or bad deed, they insist, is rewarded or punished, tit for tat, here on the physical plane of our existence. Alluding to Christ's words in Matthew 5:18, New-Agers further claim that Jesus says that every jot and tittle of the "law"—the law of karma—must be fulfilled. Actually Jesus was speaking of the law given to us through Moses and the prophets, not a law of cause and effect; but New-Agers aren't concerned, as already noted, about context. If it feels right, it must be right.

As you think, so shall you become. By extension, if every action produces an equivalent reaction, then every thought, so runs this argument, must likewise manifest its equivalent on the material plane. If I am sad, I reap sadness; if I am happy, I reap happiness. As any occultist will tell you, thoughts are things. As a result, thoughts act and react according to the law of karma, producing good or ill in one's life according to the quality of his thoughts. At this point another law is often described too—the law of attraction, a law that guarantees that whatever one consistently dwells on will come to pass—whatever one ardently yearns for will be drawn to him. With the help of the Higher Power, one will even be able to create what he desires out of the elemental substance of the universe:

> Think and feel exhaustless riches in relationships and mate-
> rial requirements, and then draw it from the *All*! You are
> wealthy beyond comprehension! You can draw a wealth of
> poverty or the fullness of life. The exhaustless riches are built
> from what you draw! This is Truth about the Self.
> —*Davies 11*

It's easy to understand the excitement that such an idea engenders, especially in a person who has felt like a victim most of his life. "At last," such a person cries and sighs, "I can be in complete control of my circumstances and my destiny. I'm free!" The fact that there is little evidence that such a law exists doesn't concern him, precisely because his hurts and disappointments make him impatient to find a cure for his ailments. On this weakness New-Age theologians prey.

Armed with these two sayings—and more—the New-Age convert can stride forth confidently. He knows that he is one of the few who understand that the engine of the universe, as well as all its cogs and wheels, is run by karma. Then, believing that every human is the master of his own fate, he concentrates on obtaining for himself not only the good life but also salvation, a salvation extended to all universally, especially if they exert themselves in the right way according to "the wisdom of the ages." From then on he can rationalize the suffering in the world and set out to create for *himself* a heaven on earth. Whether on the physical plane or on the spiritual plane, this new heaven is eternal, and its counterpart, an eternal hell, no longer exists except in the minds of "unevolved" spiritual seekers.

A DEFICIENT COSMOLOGY

There are three serious deficiencies in these three theories of maya, *prakriti*, and karma. The first concerns the nature of the law, the second, the status of God, and the third, the role of grace within God's creation.

The Cold, Impersonal Law

The law of karma, as it's said to function within maya or *prakriti*, is mechanistic and simplistic and thus untenable. The idea that we live in a perfectly ordered universe that we can fully understand, if only we will understand causality, smacks of an earlier age, the Age of Enlightenment, hearkening back to the clockwork God of the Deists, to Newtonian physics—in short, to easy answers. If we are unwary, New-Agers will convince us that their laws are scientific and certain, even though—because of the current theories of relativity and quantum mechanics, especially the uncertainty principle—few scientists today are this certain. The study of nature, these scientists tell us, no longer provides us with easy or "absolute" answers to our questions about causality.

Nevertheless, undaunted, New-Agers forge ahead, ever adaptable and flexible as the need arises. If rational proof isn't available, they will trot out their metaphysical gobbledygook about "karmic influences" and "planetary aspects," about "soul mates" and "past-life regressions." They will appeal to intuition, smiling benignly as they speculate about auras, energies, and colors. Or, using what appears to be deductive reasoning, they will quote some ancient occultic authority: "As above, so below; as below, so above" (Three Initiates 113). And they will then proffer some vague pseudo-scientific interpretation:

> The great Second Hermetic Principle embodies the truth that there is a harmony, agreement, and correspondence between the several planes of Manifestation, Life and Being. This truth is a truth because all that is included in the Universe emanates from the same source, and the same laws, principles, and characteristics apply to each unit, or combination of units of activity, as each manifests its own phenomena upon its own plane.
>
> —113

Thus with seeming erudition, they will astound their converts and put an end to all debate.

Furthermore, the idea that we can manipulate these laws, making them do our bidding, is presumptuous, if not arrogant. Here we are, puny creatures on a puny planet in a puny solar system within a puny galaxy, and some of us actually believe that we can, like Prometheus, catch and control the fire of God. Apparently, with a little occultic knowledge and systematic effort every man or woman can have, be, or do whatever he or she wants. But what happens if many "enlightened" people, many "masters," want the same object and only one of that kind exists? What happens when two thousand masters all want to be the President of the United States at the same time? Are we really wise enough to know that what we want is what we need or that what we want will be for the good of all? As usual, in New-Age circles such questions remain unasked and unanswered. In this way New-Age teachers can prey upon the naive and confused, the vainglorious and greedy.

Even worse, to conceive of the universe as a flawlessly run, well-oiled machine is callous. How do we explain the presence of starving children in Ethiopia or homeless children in the United States? "It's their karma," many New-Agers will tell us. In some past life these children neglected their own children or, as rulers or rich people, oppressed the poor people for whom they should have been responsible. As they sowed, they have reaped; as they thought, they have now become. In fact, concerning the condition of poverty, one New-Age writer has offered this answer: "A man with a poverty type mind finds himself in poverty-stricken conditions" (Murphy 106). By extension, poverty-stricken children have poverty-type minds. They are only getting what they deserve. With such rationalizations, what would induce people to feel compassion toward those in need? What beyond the enhancement of their own good karma and the purification of their own consciousness would induce them to feed and clothe the homeless or to wipe away the orphan's tears?

How would New-Agers explain the brutal murder of a kidnapped adolescent or the deaths of two hundred passengers on a crashed jumbo jet? Are these victims guilty of murders that they committed in their past lives or just of the "negative thoughts" that they entertained in their most recent life? In the case of the kidnapped adolescent, an apparently happy, good-hearted, and popular girl, it would be simpleminded at best, callous at worst, for New-Agers to suggest that she had similarly molested and strangled an innocent girl in a previous life. Such a conclusion simply can't be verified. They would also seriously stretch credulity were they to argue that she "attracted" the violence to herself through her own negative thinking. A law that would hold us responsible for our thoughts to such an extent seems unjust and pitiless in the extreme.

In the case of the victims of an airplane crash, New-Agers would have to make similar assumptions. Are we really to conclude that every man, woman, and child on that plane had pushed somebody off a cliff in a previous life or had feared flying for so long that all were mysteriously drawn together for this one accident? If we could draw such conclusions about one person or a plane-load of people, then we could just as easily draw such conclusions about even larger groups of people—say, the six million Jews who died at the hands of the Nazis during World War II. Any sensible person would have to recoil from such conclusions.

How much negative thinking, we have a right to ask, does it take to make an airplane accident or a brutal murder? How many millions of interlocking incidences of cruelty are required to lead to the decimation of a race by genocide?

The Redundancy of God

If we are entirely responsible for everything in our lives, if we can ennoble or depress ourselves through our own efforts alone, then God becomes unnecessary. A fully autonomous, self-sufficient creature would no longer need a Sovereign. Standing at the center of the universe, preoccupied with himself, such a creature would pull down out of the "ethers" or up out of his own subconscious all that he needed in the way of wisdom and material possessions. Emboldened by his grasp of the law of karma, he would command nature—including his own nature—to submit to his overarching will.

In a mechanistic, man-centered universe, the only God would be the Self. And no matter how richly this idea is adorned and ornamented, the result is narcissism. God, the very reality that many New-Agers had set out to verify, is denied altogether. If all of nature, including matter and thought, is maya, then so is the concept of a sovereign God who controls and orders his creation. As long as the New-Ager is ignorant of his True Self, he of course conditionally accepts the existence of *prakriti*, the primal substance of the universe; but he also believes that, according to the law of karma, he has an absolute right to control and direct it— to do, be, and have whatever he wants. Because he believes that his True Self is the Self of the universe, he concludes that he has the right to rule over his own creation. And he has no doubt that all of nature must yield to him. In this way, from the beginning to the end of his search, all that matters to him is his own Self.

The Impossibility of Grace

Despite the protestations of yoga-Vedantins and New-Agers at this point, their theories of the universe do indeed exclude the possibility that grace may operate in people's lives—if not theoretically, then practically. An exacting law of karma allows no room for grace.

Let me illustrate this point with a simple story that Swami S., my former guru and an orthodox yoga-Vedantin, told on several occasions. A thief, his bagful of loot in hand, was once fleeing from a mob of angry villagers. Because it was dark, he managed to elude them in the dense jungle outside the village by climbing a tree, from which, out of sight, he observed them pass, torches in hand. Just as he was thinking of climbing down from the tree, however, he spied a man in a clearing not far from him seated before a ritual fire. He was worshiping the Divine Mother, weeping and praying for one gracious glance from her, obviously longing wholeheartedly for a vision of her. Suddenly, while the thief was looking on in horror, a crouched tiger crept up behind the man, snatched him, and dragged him away into the dark jungle.

Curious, the thief scrambled down from the tree, sauntered over to the fire, and seated himself on the man's cushion of *kusha* grass. To his surprise, as soon as he attempted to perform the worship of the deity, she immediately appeared before him in all her beaded and bangled splendor, smiling graciously at him. Taken aback, he asked her why she had blessed him of all people, a thief who had never worshiped God in his life. After all, she hadn't even lifted a finger to help the other man, an obviously devout yogi and worshiper of hers. She simply replied that because of his intense spiritual efforts in his former lives he was ready for her appearance—that is, he had *earned* the right to see her fully. The other man hadn't as yet merited that privilege.

Clearly, in the New-Age universe karma must take precedence over grace, even when a person is seeking knowledge of God. After all, he can only get what he deserves according to the degree and amount of his efforts. Otherwise, if he were to get that which he hadn't earned, the law of karma wouldn't be perfectly regular or perfectly just—it wouldn't be a law. In a mechanistic universe in which God doesn't ultimately exist—except perhaps as an impersonal primal or mental substance—there can be no room for the unpredictable, and such is grace.

Yoga-Vedantins and New-Agers confirm this legalistic view over and over. Swami Vivekananda, one of the most celebrated disciples of Ramakrishna, told a group of his Western students how they could free themselves from the "bonds of imperfection": "This bondage can only fall off through the mercy of God; and this mercy comes to the pure. So purity is the *condition* of His mercy" (Vivekananda, *Inspired Talks* 210, italics mine). If purity is a condition of mercy, then the seeker must himself achieve it; if he must achieve it, then he must employ self-effort to do so. Thus self-effort is the *sine qua non* in the life of a spiritual seeker.

Another popular swami in the United States has described the law of karma in this way: "This grand law works everywhere in the physical and mental planes. No phenomenon can escape from the operation of this mighty law" (Shivananda 189). A page later he says emphatically, "This law is inexorable and immutable" (190). Even more forcefully, a New-Age writer has put it this way: "[Y]ou are the architect of your own destiny. Every experience or condition in your life—poverty or riches, success or failure, health or illness—is the result of action and purpose set in motion by you" (Williams xiii). If, after describing the human role thus, the yoga-Vedantins and New-Agers speak of grace, we can be certain that they don't mean by "grace" the same thing that Christians mean. Or they are quite willing to contradict themselves if the occasion calls for it.

And so the great wheel of the universe, with all its internal wheels and cogs, revolves; and man, ignorant of his true nature, rides it until he can no longer bear his insufferable bondage:

> This vast universe is a wheel. Upon it are all creatures that are subject to birth, death, and rebirth. Round and round it turns, and never stops. It is the wheel of Brahman. As long as the individual self thinks it is separate from Brahman, it revolves upon the wheel in bondage to the laws.
>
> —*Upanishads* 118

And where is God in this scenario—the God of Abraham, Isaac, Jacob, and Jesus? Nowhere to be found. The New-Age and yoga-Vedantic cosmology is grounded in natural, not supernatural, religion. It's as ancient as the first lie—that man is wise enough to survive and thrive outside the will of an Almighty God.

4

THE MANY
SONS OF GOD

It is God Himself who is sporting in the form of man.
—Ramakrishna, M. 392

SEVERAL YEARS AGO A NEW-AGE FRIEND WAS TELLING ME
how impressed she was with a husband-and-wife team who
were teachers of something called Alpha Dynamics. With this
new system they had found a way to raise their mental vibrations
to such an elevated pitch that they were capable of perceiving and
manipulating psychic forces. Driven by the desire to spread the
good news, they were teaching other people how to reach this
same advanced, receptive state of mind. As evidence of their high
achievements, my friend cited an example of the woman's most
impressive achievement. She had used the system to reach the
alpha state, tap into a higher power, and enlarge her breasts by
two sizes.

Needless to say, I was impressed, but not by the woman's feat.
Many times during the past twenty years I have heard New-Agers
lay claim to such miraculous abilities. They could, so they
claimed, levitate, read auras, predict the future infallibly, heal ailments at sixty paces. Constantly extolling the powers of man,
they would hold out to me endless possibilities. If only I could
identify the hidden power within my subconscious or the Christ
Self within me, I too could create a new heaven and earth for
myself. By practicing some new method or system, I too could

evolve spiritually into a higher order of being. No, I wasn't impressed by the woman's accomplishment but by something else: the triviality of her goal and the shallowness of the mind that had conceived it.

As a rule New-Agers, Western occultists as well as yoga-Vedantins, are made of nobler stuff. True, they almost always extol self-effort and cater to those who desire prestige and power, whether of the material or spiritual sort. But the sincere among them also talk about the need to promote the common good, to advance the cause of human welfare. They admire self-sacrifice and virtue, at least as a means to a spiritual end. They revere the life and teachings of Jesus Christ and other "great masters." And they strive for their high-minded goals with an impressive zeal.

Nevertheless, when they consider man as a body and a soul, as free, unsullied spirit encased in gross matter, something in their theology goes awry. They lapse into queer distortions about the nature and potential of man, some of which we have already touched upon in earlier chapters. Usually, however, these distortions follow one of two primary lines of thought. Either psycho-physical needs and desires are to be sublimated and transcended so the yogis can identify themselves with spirit alone; or psycho-physical needs and desires are to be refined and fulfilled, according to the law of karma, so the occultists can become masters of themselves and their circumstances here on earth or, later, "ascended masters" in "higher realms." When one follows the first line of development, austerity is the method and pure spirituality is the fruit; when one follows the second, mind control is the method and material abundance is the fruit. In the end, both are supposed to lead to self-mastery and enlightenment. Both, however, represent false extremes based on a fundamental misconception about man.

THE NEW-AGE CONCEPTION OF MAN

If God is real and the universe is illusory, then it follows that the true self in man is real and the body is illusory. "[T]he self is all" (*Upanishads* 27); the body, at best, is a vehicle or instrument for the soul's self-expression and, more important, its evolutionary climb toward God-consciousness. In short, the body has little value except as a means to an end. New-Age theology, as a look at Eastern and Western sources will bear out, results in a radical rupture not only between the body and soul but also between man and God.

Yoga-Vedanta

In the "Katha Upanishad," the relationship between the Self and the body is explained in this way:

> Know that the Self is the rider, and the body the chariot; that the intellect is the charioteer, and the mind the reins.
>
> The senses, say the wise, are the horses; the roads they travel are the mazes of desire. The wise call the Self the enjoyer when he is united with the body, the senses, and the mind.
>
> When a man lacks discrimination and his mind is uncontrolled, his senses are unmanageable, like the restive horses of a charioteer. But when a man has discrimination and his mind is controlled, his senses, like the well-broken horses of a charioteer, lightly obey the rein.
>
> —Upanishads 19

Seen in this light, the body, a chariot, is to the Self what an inanimate object is to a human rider. The intellect is perceived to be the controlling agent, the driver. As the faculty of discrimination, it must constantly distinguish the Self from the not-Self, the Real from the unreal. But the mind itself is also likened to an inanimate object—reins, and the senses are regarded as beasts of burden—well-broken horses. Together, then, the body, mind, and senses represent inferior, expendable objects.

As we all know, horses are usually broken by force. And indeed the yogi intent on realizing God must struggle hard to whip his body, mind, and senses into shape. To this end, he practices various disciplines, the "eight limbs of yoga": *yama* and *niyama* (austerities whose aim is virtue, purity, and self-control); *asana* (posture); *pratyahara* and *dharana* (control of the mind and senses; concentration); *pranayama* (breath control); *dhyana* (meditation); and *samadhi* (absorption in the Self). Through such practices, the yogi gains various powers, ranging from being able to see into the past and future to being able to enter the body of another person (Patanjali 97ff.; 126ff.). In the end the yogi becomes omnipotent and omniscient. He is liberated from his gross and troublesome bondage to his body, mind, and senses. He becomes the Self, discovering that he has always been the Self.

But the great monistic Vedantin Shankaracharya has made the relationship between the body and Self even clearer. To him also, "the body is merely a vehicle of experience for the human spirit" (Shankara, *Crest Jewel* 46). That is, it's an inferior, expendable object. At the same time, however, for Shankara the body is something foul and disgusting, something beneath our contempt. "O fool," he cries, "stop identifying yourself with this lump of skin, flesh, fat, bones, and filth" (Shankara, *Crest Jewel* 57). Realization of the Self, on the other hand, leads to a true assessment of reality. The liberated person, freed from his terrible bondage to ignorance, asserts the truth:

> I am the soul of the universe. I am all things, and above all things. I am one without a second. I am pure consciousness, single and universal. I am joy. I am life everlasting.
> —*107*

Thus, by denigrating and rejecting psycho-physical existence, the monistic Vedantin attains to the knowledge that his True Self alone exists.

Western Occultism

In a similar way, from Madame Blavatsky to Edgar Cayce, from Manly P. Hall to Elizabeth Clare Prophet, New-Agers refer to the body as a vehicle or instrument. "To the occultist," says Yogi Ramacharaka, a Westerner with a Hindu aka, "the physical body is merely a temporary vehicle for the soul which the latter discards at the proper time" (*Mystic Christianity* 178). Like an old car, the body is apparently to be discarded for a new one as the occultist continues on his evolutionary journey. And what is the purpose and end of this journey? "The objective of the evolutionary process," according to Alice A. Bailey, "is to enhance and deepen the control of the soul over this instrument. When this is complete, we have a divine incarnation" (Bailey 51). Hence, everyone eventually becomes a son (or daughter) of God, a christ, an avatar.

After aeons of spiritual disciplines and occultic practices, the soul discovers and unleashes the Divine Self within itself, at last transcending "the muck and mire of earth-life," as Ramacharaka puts it. Referring to the Hindu god Indra, who assumed the form of a pig and then forgot his true nature, Ramacharaka goes on to explain the New-Age or "mystical" interpretation of Christian salvation:

> It is to bring you to a realization that you are a god and not a pig, that Jesus, the Master, is working within your soul as the Christ Principle. Have you never heard His voice, crying from within your soul, "Come out—come out of your pig-nature and realize the god that you really are!"
> —190-91

Here renunciation is taken to the extreme. We aren't merely supposed to love God and so turn our minds and hearts toward godliness. We are supposed to detest and despise all things physical and material. In doing so, of course, we are forgetting that God created our bodies and our world and that he, upon creating them, pronounced them good. Here, in this denigration of the body and all things material, we encounter the remnants of a Gnosticism that the Church long ago discarded—and for good reason.

In both the East and West, New-Agers have developed elaborate systems to explain the relationship of the body to the soul and the means by which the soul is to be freed from the body. They refer to various subtle bodies within the corporeal body itself—the astral body, the mental body, and so on. Or they refer to sheaths or veils that cover the soul, ranging from the grossest to the subtlest substances. While practicing austerities and meditation, the yoga-Vedantin, for example, must destroy his identification with various *koshas* or sheaths—the body, the mind, the intellect, the ego—to discover his real nature. Even in this life he is supposed to be able to realize God—that is, to see and become one with God. As we shall see, elaborate spiritual systems are always necessary when man, attached to his natural religion, attempts to reach God by his own efforts.

The Mighty Fulcrum of Self-effort

No concept of man can be complete without a consideration of his condition in relation to God. Religion starts from the premise that man has somehow become separated from his source of life and wisdom—namely, God. According to Christians, it's sin that separates man from God. Man falsely believes that he can exist without God, that he can be a law unto himself. The sin, then, is one of pride and self-will. To New-Agers, both in the East and the West, however, ignorance, not sin, separates man from God.

Clinging to the illusion of separateness, they say, man lives as though he were one thing and God another when in fact man and God are essentially the same. According to them, man has the power to liberate himself from this illusion of separateness, if only he will struggle hard to realize his True Self. Thus to New-Agers self-will is a virtue.

The spirituality that derives from such an assumption about the condition of man must necessarily be man-centered and self-congratulatory. Therefore, I call it "a macho spirituality," a spirituality that begins, proceeds, and ends in self-effort. Such a path requires self-reliance, boldness, even arrogance, because the spiritual aspirant must believe in his own powers and in the infallibility of the law of karma. As a result, he will be constantly on the lookout for experiences that confirm his spiritual progress. For some, past-life recall or astral projections will suffice. For others, the manifestation of their visualized desires—in the form of possessions, job status, or enduring relationships—will satisfy this desire. For still others, nothing less than peace of mind, universal love, or "God-realization," however momentary, will confirm their spiritual progress.

Among these latter, especially, there are many who pride themselves on their self-discipline. "I meditate every morning for an hour," says one. "Well, I meditate twice a day, in the morning for two and a half hours and in the evening for an hour," says another, while a third remains silent, his back as straight as a rod, his eyes focused on nothing, testifying to his high spiritual state. For such people as these, there is no greater joy than flexing their spiritual muscles.

To reinforce this emphasis on experience, yoga-Vedantic and Western occultic teachers speak of "spiritual evolution," referring often to different "stages of development" or different "levels of consciousness." They show reverence toward their "sages" or "ascended masters" by extolling their "high level of consciousness." They show their tolerance toward Christians or Jews by hinting that they are "at a lower level of consciousness." "But that's all right," one New-Age teacher used to say to me, because "that's just where they're at." Of course, such an appeal to spiritual grades allows yoga-Vedantic and New-Age teachers to rank themselves and others according to a hierarchy of "experiences." Thus the master, who is so identified with the One that he can uplift or heal others with a mere glance, occupies the top rung of the ladder. And the devotee of "the personal God"—a Christian, for example—occupies the lowest rung. He is a mere spiritual baby who needs concrete proofs and highly charged emotional experiences to help him keep his feet planted firmly on the spiritual path. But someday, when he becomes spiritually mature, he will understand the Truth as taught by the yoga-Vedantins and Western occultists.

One alleged avatar has even suggested that the less spiritually evolved devotee actually creates the personhood of God for himself out of the pure, absolute substance of Brahman:

> To a devotee God manifests Himself in various forms. Just think of a shoreless ocean—an infinite expanse of water—no land visible in any direction; only here and there are visible blocks of ice formed by intense cold. Similarly, under the cooling influence . . . of the deep devotion of His worshipper, the Infinite reduces Himself into the Finite and appears before him as a Being with form. Again, as on the appearance of the sun, the ice melts away, so on the appearance of the sun of knowledge, God with form melts away into the formless.
>
> —*Ramakrishna 8-9*

Thus knowledge is higher than devotion, the impersonal Infinite greater than God the Person. According to this line of thinking, God is an illusion that we devise for ourselves while we are yet ignorant of the Truth, while we are yet in the kindergarten of our spiritual life. When we become grown-ups, then we will understand that Brahman, the True Self, alone exists. In agreement with the yoga-Vedantins, the New-Agers of every kind chortle, "I am that I AM," once again wrenching a biblical quotation out of its context—the words of Yahweh, no less, the Personal God.

Because proud man has always enjoyed erecting great and elaborate structures, a man-centered religion of this kind must necessarily be characterized by many different systems and methods. If the spiritual seeker is to follow a well-marked, ascending path, there must be certain practices that he can adopt to ensure his progress. Here natural religion—with all its various sages, masters, spirit guides, initiates, and so on—provides the spiritual seeker with a plethora of much-desired directions.

The seeker has only to select from a vast array of choices the method that appeals to him. Should he follow Ouspensky and Gurdjieff, Rajneesh or Muktananda, Yogananda or Ramakrishna, Aurobindo or Satchitananda, Sai Baba or Meher Baba, Elizabeth Clare Prophet or Charles Fillmore? Should he join The Divine Light Mission, Eckankar, the Order of the Adytum, the Rosicrucians, the Theosophists, or the A.R.E.? Or, like a true individualist, should he, eschewing all organizations, consult all or some of these sources and devise his own method or system? The possibilities are endless for the ardent seeker of truth. Some seekers choose one teacher or system. Most, however, trusting their Higher Self and their own intuitions, prefer the smorgasbord approach, selecting their methods according to their prevailing tastes. A former yoga-Vedantin friend of mine, personally familiar with this approach, once aptly referred to it as "Temple hopping." Certain practices, however, are common to most of the groups.

PHYSICAL DISCIPLINES.   New-Age physical disciplines have as their goal the subjugation of the body and the attainment of purity. Consider hatha yoga, a widely accepted form of exercise in America. People think of hatha yoga as simply a means by which one can obtain and maintain good health, youthful vigor, peace of mind, and so on. And yet hatha yoga is grounded in yoga philosophy. Traditionally it has been practiced in conjunction with the eight limbs of yoga—*yama, niyama, asana,* and so on—the goal of which, as we have already seen, is self-mastery, liberation, and God-consciousness as defined by the yoga-Vedantins. When beaming New-Agers, their clothes saturated with the scent of sandalwood incense, twist and stretch their bodies into fantastic poses, they are participating in the yogic tradition. They learn how to master their muscles and bodily functions, to purge their bodies of impurities, and to purify and calm their nervous systems so they can turn inward and gaze upon the Godhead within, seeing him clearly within their newly self-clarified minds.

For this same reason, some will adopt sexual and dietary prohibitions. Hindus have long regarded the attachments to the tongue and sexual organs as the greatest impediments to the attainment of God-consciousness. The earnest spiritual seeker, therefore, must control these organs and redirect the energies that they waste toward the spiritual goal. Celibacy is urged upon the yogi because it is said not only to conserve energy but to build up a subtle form of energy, called *ojas* by yoga-Vedantins. This *ojas,* a kind of psychical fuel, aids the yogi in his spiritual endeavors. Similarly, the spiritual seeker often feels inclined to become a vegetarian because meat, he is told, is impure (Yukteswar 41-45). It pollutes and destroys the body, lowers one's level of consciousness, and, according to one learnéd New-Ager whom I once knew, attracts to the seeker gross spiritual entities from the lower planes of consciousness. Obviously this is *not* good. (Besides, if the yogi isn't careful, he may end up eating his deceased grandmother, who in her current life is serving a probationary sentence as a milk cow.)

Even moral culture is undertaken so that the spiritual seeker may gradually free himself from gross desires and thus refine his mind. He renounces his love for money and pleasure so he can check the outward movement of his senses toward objects. On the one hand, he wants to protect himself from worldly contamination. By doing so he becomes "pure," and by becoming "pure" he knows that he will see the glory of his Self more clearly reflected in his soul. On the other hand, he wants perfect self-control; he wants to harness all his physical powers—indeed, all the power in the universe. The Higher Power can then begin to flow into and through him once he transcends his sense of physical limitation—an illusion created, he believes, by his wayward, restive senses and his physical passions.

For the truly stalwart seeker, this indifference toward pleasures may entail the renunciation of even legitimate desires. Because he wishes to overcome the likes and dislikes of the illusory self, he eschews all interest in a career, filial loyalty, marriage, parenthood, friendships, and so on. He wants to remain detached and to avoid worldly entanglements as much as possible. Marriage, parenthood, career—all these, he feels, lead to bondage and perpetuate his ignorance. A macho spirituality, then, calls for the control of one's senses, the eradication of all desires, and the annihilation of the ego—the sense of *I, me,* and *mine.* It's radical and uncompromising.

> If there is a small hole in the bottom of a jar of water, the whole water flows out by and by; similarly, if there be the slightest tinge of worldliness [that is, desire or egoism] in the aspirant, all his [spiritual] exertions come to naught.
> —*Ramakrishna 48*

The hole can only be shored up if the spiritual aspirant refuses to let his senses become attached to the objects of desire. If he must live among the worldly, then he is supposed to remain dispassionate, unmoved by the flickering pictures of maya projected by

Brahman and superimposed upon Brahman by his own ignorance. Like the rider in the chariot, he must whip his horses into
shape and keep them galloping toward God-consciousness.

MENTAL DISCIPLINES.   In this strenuous effort to master the
self, the serious spiritual seeker also practices mind control,
called raja yoga by the yoga-Vedantins. He will sit motionless,
staring at a flickering candle, or concentrate on a point above and
between his eyebrows—the ajna or "third eye," as it has been
called by Western occultists. Or he will urge forth the *kundalini,*
the coiled serpent power locked up at the base of his spine. In one
way or another he must gain control of his mind, still its waves,
the *chittavrittis,* and lose himself in his True Self. In time the yogi
will become a miracle-worker able to manifest objects out of
nowhere, to see into the future, to appear and disappear at will,
to even raise the dead. All powers come to the yogi who is per-
sistent.

In the West, spiritual seekers rely on similar disciplines. Some
in the New-Age Movement, of course, adopt the yogic methods,
learning to empty and concentrate their minds. A few turn to
Western Occultism and meditate on tarot or medicine cards,
seeking integration. But most tend to use positive affirmations
and creative visualization to tap into their Higher Power and
unleash their "spiritual potential." Like autosuggestion, affirmations and prayer formulas are believed to reprogram the subconscious mind, making it positive and powerful. As the
New-Ager begins to serve as a "channel" for the Higher Power,
he then employs creative visualization to help him become a co-
creator with God. He focuses all his energies on his mental picture of success and then attempts to let the Higher Power sweep
through him and project his picture onto the real world. In theory he is supposed to "manifest" his desired object—say, a
Cadillac—by picturing it, empowering his picture with the infu-

sion of the Higher Power and bending all his efforts toward obtaining his object of desire, even to the point of obsession (consult, for example, Napoleon Hill's *Think and Grow Rich*).

For those who love novelty, several other practices are available. Thousands flock to teachers of all kinds who initiate them, usually for a considerable fee, into the mysteries of astral projection, past-life regressions, or dream analysis. Here, too, are to be found all the "therapies": Gestalt, Reichean, Rolfian, polarity, and so on. Most of the lovers of novelty are on the fringes of the movement and usually have no well-developed theology, even though they can parrot the standard New-Age assumptions and objections to Christianity. They are content to feel good—to be titillated.

SPIRITUAL DISCIPLINES. In the East, there are two fundamental ways by which one can reach God: *jnana yoga*—the path of knowledge, and *bhakti yoga*—the path of devotion. The jnani uses the sharp sword of discrimination to distinguish the Real from the unreal—the Atman, his True Self, from maya—so that he can constantly affirm his identity with the Atman. Usually such a yogi takes to the path of renunciation, internal as well as external, as the only means by which he can achieve success: "One must have both internal and external Sannyasa—renunciation in spirit as well as formal renunciation" (Chakravarty 220-21). "Without dispassion for the world, without renunciation, without giving up the desire for enjoyment," says the same swami, "*absolutely nothing* can be accomplished in the spiritual life" (221, italics mine).

The bhakta, on the other hand worships his *Ishta*, the personal form of God that he has chosen for himself: Krishna, Rama, Shiva, Kali, and so on. Through rituals and devotions, through intense love for his ideal deity or *Ishta devata*, he eventually progresses from the concrete forms of worship to the subtle forms, from self-exertion to self-surrender, from the many to the One. At last, we are told, he becomes established in God-consciousness, just as surely as the jnani does. According to many yoga-Vedantins, however, in the end the bhakta will have to take to the path of jnana yoga, for knowledge of God, to them, is higher than the love of God.

In the West, although New-Agers love to use the yogic terms and concepts to lend credibility to their discussions, their spiritual disciplines are far less well defined. Essentially, New-Agers are simply urged to have faith in themselves and their Higher Power. Beyond that faith, almost anything is permissible: if the practice feels good, they adopt it. And New-Age gurus are constantly creating new methods. One of these teachers some years ago taught the people in his class an elaborate meditation on Jesus Christ that involved lying on one's back and imagining Jesus lying on his back, the soles of Jesus' feet pressed against the soles of the meditator's feet. Still others talk about creating "bubbles of love" as protection against "negative influences" or projecting rays of healing love to their friends and enemies to bring peace and love into the world. A few occult groups recommend daily meditations on the Higher Power or spiritual centers (the yogic *chakras*) in the body; but their disciplines and routines are unappealing, as a rule, to the average New-Ager, who wants success, wealth, health, and pleasure rather than spiritual enlightenment.

A FLAWED ANTHROPOLOGY

The Denigration of the Body

As we have seen, yoga-Vedantins and Western New-Agers liken the body to a vehicle or instrument. Seen in this light, the body is an expendable object, not the temple of the living God, even though New-Agers will sometimes misleadingly and hypocritically refer to it as such. This denigration of the body as a limiting adjunct of the soul leads away from the real, commonsensical world that we all inhabit toward two falsely conceived worlds.

First, there is the "other side," consisting of various "planes" and "levels of being," including wise and not-so-wise spirits, the astral plane, and so on, devoid, as a rule, of any organized evil. From this world, their true home, they garner all their wisdom as it comes to them through meditation, trance mediums, or spiritually experienced gurus. And whenever they are questioned about the legitimacy of their otherworldly aims and truths, they simply appeal to the authority of their subjective experiences and deny that any objective truths exist. In this way they deny the mind and body a real place in the education of the soul. As a merely temporary vehicle with only questionable existence and value, the "psycho-physical organism" can't really be cherished as a unique creation of God. Nor can it be seen as having a purpose in God's plan to reestablish his kingdom on earth. After all, it's scrapped like a totaled Toyota at death so the seeker can continue on his way—first, to pass through a tunnel of light into his world of ascended masters; next, to reincarnate to assume a new vehicle. Therefore, what such a seeker wants, above all else, is to receive insights from the "other world," not gain wisdom in this world.

Then there is the "material plane," the other falsely conceived world, regarded as a creation of maya or one's own mind. For yoga-Vedantins and some New-Agers, this illusory, unpredictable world is to be renounced and transcended. For most New-Agers, however, the material world, as they conceive of it, is to be mastered. Because it's the creation of the mind, it's conquerable, at least to the extent that they can summon up and rely upon their "mind powers." New-Agers dwell, therefore, in a material world of endless possibilities, in which all limitations can be denied and all desires can be fulfilled. In this world the New-Age seeker is well-nigh omnipotent, capable of being, doing, and having anything he wants as long as he attunes himself to his Higher Power, visualizes his goals, and works hard to make them "manifest." Those of us who can't experience the joy of positive thinking, those of us who actually agonize over moral distinctions and rejoice in our dependence on Christ—finding strength in our weakness—are obviously ignorant and worldly-minded. They call our values mundane, our outlook "unevolved."

Three errors, I believe, result from this denigration of the body—and, indeed, of all things physical. First, reason, as it has been understood traditionally, no longer has value in the New-Age world. Open to all manner of new experiences for the sake of novelty, New-Agers refuse to reason inductively (from specific examples to general principles) or deductively (from general principles to specific examples). If something feels right, they embrace it. Hence, they are anti-rational and subjectivistic. In fact, in the worst sense of the term, they are *dogmatic*—that is, stubbornly closed-minded. They insist on the reality and absolute authority of their own private insights and visions, even when these contradict reason, common sense, and reality. When confronted with well-reasoned arguments and proofs, they smile benignly yet condescendingly.

Second, the real nature of the world, with all its sinfulness and injustice, is ignored and even denied. In the New-Age world, no sins exist; no limitations are allowed. New-Agers are convinced that all the innovations in "lifestyles" and entertainment during the past forty years are all signs of progression—namely, evolution. To them, all change that conforms to their agenda is good. They can't even entertain the possibility that the sexual revolution, for example, has wrought more evil than good in our society. That gays have come out of the closet, that movie stars now bare all in films, that teens demand that condoms be distributed to them on their high-school campuses—all these phenomena, according to such people, are signs that we are being liberated from our benighted Judeo-Christian past. The farther we move away from the Judeo-Christian worldview and ethic and the closer we edge toward moral relativism and individual empowerment, the more they become convinced that the New Age is about to dawn.

Moreover, New-Agers can't believe that poverty can come to people who have "rightly" sought wealth or that unhappiness can come to people who have "rightly" sought happiness. They can't believe, in other words, that one can think the "right" way and take the "right" steps and still end up poor, unhappy, or sick. Like the woman above who raised her consciousness and increased the size of her breasts, they have an infantile need to believe in their own omnipotence in a world in which there are few, if any, guarantees. If they fail to achieve their selfish ends, then, according to them, they either lacked faith or they failed to understand and apply the law of attraction, an offshoot of the law of karma, as they should have. They just weren't "ready" yet for the blessings they sought.

Finally, the need for human sympathy, the capacity to suffer when others suffer, is minimized and sometimes discarded in favor of a worldview that holds that each person always gets what he deserves. By holding such a view, New-Agers can turn their backs on two-thirds of the people of the earth. People suffer because it's their karma to suffer. Like Hindus who have been reared on The *Upanishads*, New-Agers come to believe, as Dinesh D'Souza puts it, "that it is a waste of time to combat social injustice, as true liberation comes from the inner soul's receptivity to the divine calling" ("A Multicultural Reading List," *Wall Street Journal*, September 24, 1991). Therefore, it's up to the "ignorant" suffering masses to free themselves. When they can abandon their illusions and attain to the "higher view" of life, they too will be able to hearken to the divine calling within and manipulate the law of karma to their own advantage. Until then, they are lost.

Of course, the New-Ager realizes that he can serve these

unfortunate souls, but he can't impart to them the higher truths until they are "ready." In the meantime, he can patiently worship God, the True Self, in those benighted souls and earn good karma for himself in the process. As a center of divine power, he knows that through his thoughts, words, and deeds he is really uplifting humanity by merely treading upon his own path. In his own mind, he is God's gift to the world.

The Advance of the Spiritual Elite

What presumption, what bigotry the New-Agers submit to when they believe they are part of a spiritual elite, highly developed according to their levels of consciousness—namely, according to their agreement with New-Age conceptions! In subscribing to this worldview, they fall prey to pride and vanity, the very sins that alienate us from God. If they believe there are spiritual grades of evolution, then who among them can resist the temptation to compare themselves favorably with others, especially with the less enlightened? God may, indeed, be active in all human vehicles, but some vehicles, New-Agers will tell us, are more aware of their true relationship to God than are most others. Through spiritual evolution, someday the "worldly minded" will become "spiritually minded." Then they, too, will join the spiritual elite, destined to achieve God-consciousness the New-Age way.

Such ideas smack of a spiritual fascism. If New-Agers conceive of themselves as spiritually superior to the majority of humans, then they aren't so far from the rationalizations of Nietzsche about his supermen or of Hitler about his Aryan race. It's their duty to do what is right for the rest of us less evolved souls—to decry the "hypocrisy" of Christian pastors, to drive Christian prayer from our schools, to teach children and adults how to center themselves and meditate transcendentally. How else are they going to usher in the New Age with its generic religion, its metaphysical gobbledygook, and its faith in the unlimited spiritual potential and perfectibility of man? They, so they think, are the true benefactors of mankind. Who else can do the job?

Is it any wonder, then, that these New-Age seekers have difficulty receiving the message of the Church—namely, that salvation comes by grace through faith in Jesus Christ? As long as they cling to their faith in the True Self and in the law of karma, they can't possibly grasp the meaning and intent of Paul's words: "For it is by grace you have been saved, through faith . . . not by works, so that no one can boast" (Eph. 2:8-9). As long as one feels he is a member of a spiritual elite, he will boast; and as long as he boasts, he must stand apart from Christ's saving faith. Sad to say, he stands condemned because of his much-vaunted self-righteousness and self-confidence.

The Dethronement of God

If every soul is Christ in the making, ignorant but not sinful, and if every soul is divine by nature, having God, his True Self, already at the core of his being, then external authority and objective truth become meaningless. To be sure, the spiritual seeker will consult his "experts" on "ancient wisdom," as it's called; but he will decide how he will believe and whom he will believe. His own judgment and intuition, then, become his guides. These subjective faculties, not God, occupy the central position in his life. But the truth is, God, the Supreme Other, is objective—that is, he really exists apart from our subjective experience of him. His existence isn't contingent upon our belief in him. We give him rule over our hearts by accepting his objective reality, having faith in him, and conforming ourselves to his will, which, again, he has expressed for us objectively. True, the subjective dimension is there—after we have submitted to God; but it's secondary to sacred Scripture, tradition, and right reason. So who or what is at the center of the New-Ager's life? The self—the feted, pampered, rebellious self.

When one acknowledges the objectivity of God's truth, he will necessarily have to use his mind, body, and senses to perceive, understand, and practice that truth. He will consult Scripture, take guidance from his pastor, examine orthodox teachings, and study nature. However, he will also pray to the God in whose image he was made, knowing that God abides in him through the saving grace of Christ and yet transcends nature—and the self—altogether. Therefore, to such a one, the body isn't an expendable object, and God—not one's intuition or judgment—must be trusted. This person lives by faith in the Son of God. To become good (righteous) and even holy (sanctified), he relies not on self-effort but on grace, for he knows that "if righteousness could be gained through the law [Mosaic *or* karmic], Christ died for nothing!" (Gal. 2:21).

By contrast, New-Agers are constantly searching for new techniques and higher experiences. Eager and naive, they place their faith in systems devised by men, in systems that allow for the greatest possible "freedom" for the individual to choose his own practices and arrive at his own truths. Thus, New-Agers place their faith in anti-rational, subjectivistic, man-centered methods—in short, in natural religion. Then, glassy-eyed and overconfident, they wait for those satisfying subjective clicks that will pry open the secrets of the universe for them so they, too, can master their physical vehicles and become divine incarnations or avatars—at last finding themselves, so they believe, on the same "plane of consciousness" as Jesus Christ.

Yet in and through their spiritual systems and methods, they are plainly fooled by their false faith in man. In this way they submit to the oldest sin known to man: pride. They fail to perceive the single lie that lies at the root of their systems and methods. In their New Age, God isn't manifesting himself as man; man is masquerading as God.

5

SNAPSHOTS OF THE SUN: THE RELATIVITY OF TRUTH

A S WE HAVE SEEN IN THE PRECEDING CHAPTERS, THE purveyors of New-Age theology appeal to the authority of their own experiences whenever they promote their "spiritual truths." How can anyone be sure that God is his True Self? How can he be sure that the universe is maya and that the Higher Power already resides within him to be tapped and put to his own uses? How can he be sure that he lives many lives, at the end of which he merges into the Absolute? The "masters," New-Agers tell us, have directly experienced these truths, and each person must experience them for himself—at the core of his being, in the laboratory of his own consciousness. "Verification," says Vivekananda, "is the only proof of religious truth. Each must verify for himself" (*Inspired Talks* 26). There, within our own subjectivity, we will find the ultimate truth about ourselves: "My consciousness and your consciousness are God's Consciousness! We are the Creative Spirit in Its aspect of both the One and the Many" (Davies 22). As always, "*Aham Brahmasmi*"—"I am God. You are God. Everything is God."

SUBJECTIVISM

Subjectivism is the only word that can be used to describe the theory that underlies such an approach to spiritual truth.

Philosophically speaking, subjectivism is the "theory that all knowledge is subjective and relative, never objective" (*Webster's*). Because some New-Agers might object to the use of the word *all* before *knowledge*, it would perhaps be best, for our purposes, to add before the word *knowledge* the word *spiritual*. Hard-headed, pragmatic people would recoil from the idea that their knowledge of science or business is always subjectively derived, but they would certainly agree that spiritual truth is subjectively derived. Why? Because they are realists when it comes to "the material plane," but pie-eyed idealists when it comes to "the spiritual plane."

When it comes to things spiritual, New-Agers quickly abandon reason and common sense in favor of the authority of their subjective "experiences." As a result, however, many find it difficult to apply the truths and standards of the "spiritual" to the material world. The pragmatic ones keep their metaphysical beliefs to themselves, tucked safely away in a corner of their minds while they are engaging with the world. The idealistic ones become "space cases," ill equipped to handle practical realities. After all, what person could live a conventional life while reading auras, trusting psychic impressions, basing decisions on planetary alignments, communicating with disincarnate souls on the "other side," and believing that he is the radiant center of all life in the universe?

Ethically speaking, subjectivism "considers the supreme good to be some form of subjective feeling . . . or measures supreme good by the criterion of such feeling" (*Webster's*). New-Agers trust their feelings and intuitions when they are seeking not only spiritual truths but also solutions to moral dilemmas. Ralph Waldo Emerson, one of the early American gurus of the New-Age Movement, has perhaps expressed this attitude and approach best:

I remember an answer which when quite young I was prompted to make to a valued adviser who was wont to importune me with the dear old doctrines of the church. On my saying, "What have I to do with the sacredness of traditions, if I live wholly from within?" my friend suggested, "But these impulses may be from below, not from above." I replied, "They do not seem to me to be such; but if I am the Devil's child, I will live then from the Devil." No law can be sacred to me but that of my nature. Good and bad are but names very readily transferable to that or this; the only right is after my constitution; the only wrong what is against it. A man is to carry himself in the presence of all opposition as if every thing were titular and ephemeral but he.

—"Self-Reliance" 149-50

In less eloquent but more modern terms, today's subjectivists would be more likely to say, "Do your own thing" or perhaps "Go with your feelings." In effect, the subjectivist, no matter what his persuasion, is declaring that he is his own and only authority. He heeds his own impulses, perceiving them to be sacred and denying the value and existence of objective truth.

Both in a theoretical and practical sense, then, New-Age theology is stubbornly subjectivistic. Theoretically it asserts that God, as pure consciousness, already exists within each of us as our True Self. For this reason, all wisdom, knowledge, and power are ours already. Only our ignorance keeps us from becoming spiritual giants. New-Age theology also asserts that each of us, aided by the law of karma, is capable of reaching God through his own exertions. In this regard, we are thoroughly self-sufficient and self-reliant. We need only look intently within ourselves. True, we may selectively take inspiration from others, according to our tastes and inclinations; but ultimately we are the masters of our own destinies, the captains of our own souls.

Practically speaking, this subjectivistic theology sets people free to be laws unto themselves. They may then dogmatically declare, "If I experience it and it feels good, it must be true because all truth resides in me." No one can debate with a New-

Ager if he harbors this underlying assumption about himself. But if one were to try to push the issue, he is likely to encounter in the New-Ager another assumption about truth: "Your truth is your truth and my truth is my truth"; or more precisely, "No truths are truer or greater than the truths that you or I find individually within ourselves, even when those truths differ." Here all rational discussion must end. The New-Ager continues to reign supreme in his subjective universe, undaunted by those of us who are still struggling upward, like slimy mollusks, from "the lower levels of consciousness."

Such subjectivistic assumptions lead to two unorthodox conclusions. First, because God resides within each person, no one really needs to be saved. When New-Agers are told they must be saved, they usually respond, their faces twisted in quizzical disbelief, "Saved from what?" Remember, to them ignorance, not sin, is the only barrier to the Truth that already exists, *in toto*, within them. Second, because their True Self is fully accessible to them by means of spiritual disciplines, God's grace is illusory and unnecessary. Indeed, for this reason the God of Abraham, Isaac, Jacob, and Jesus is to them a mere fiction, a limited reading, at best, of their all-inclusive Higher Power.

RELATIVISM

The natural consequence of subjectivism is relativism—"the theory of ethics or knowledge that maintains that the basis of judgment is relative, differing according to events, persons, etc." (*Webster's*). In fact, as surely as Eve sprang from Adam's rib, relativism has sprung from subjectivism, although in this case this unnatural mutation was the result of human pride rather than divine fiat. Ungodly subjectivism can't exist without its ungodly consort, relativism.

Of course, this wedding of subjectivism and relativism isn't new to the West, nor is it an exclusively Western phenomenon.

Yet when Thomas Hobbes in *Leviathan* (1651) declared that moral laws are man-made, not God-given, he not only reintroduced the modern world to materialism, but also cracked open a Pandora's box of subjectivism and relativism. If morality is man-made, then morality must be indistinguishable from opinion. Therefore, as men differ, so do their morals. If such is the case, then every man must be his own authority when it comes to morals. Other thinkers continued to propel us in the same direction: Hume (with his morality as a subjective sense), Rousseau (with his noble savage), Kant (with his categorical imperative), Hegel (with his dialectic), Mill (with his greatest happiness principle), Darwin (with his scientific proof that Hobbes was right), Nietzsche (with his amoral superman), Freud (with his pleasure principle), Dewey (with his pluralism), Russell (with his scientific atheism), Sartre (with his meaningless universe), Skinner (with his behaviorism), and a bevy of other thinkers, major and minor.

Am I oversimplifying? I don't think so. It's hard to deny that ever since the Romantic Era we have largely remained Romantics, exalting and trusting our own feelings, taking our private "trips," seeking our own self-fulfillment and truth, abiding by our situational ethics. And New-Agers have flourished in this fertile soil.

A certain Eastern mystic, however, a son of India—the land where the sun of subjectivity never sets—has expressed this relativistic view in perhaps the most poetic and modern terms possible, in terms that New-Agers, especially, will find attractive. In words that remind us that he has read Hegel and that he has imbibed the optimism of the Romantics, he creates a bridge between Western philosophy and Eastern mysticism, between the theory of evolution and New-Age theology:

> You must remember that humanity travels not from error to truth, but from truth to truth—it may be, if you like bet-

ter, from lower truth to higher truth; but never from error to truth. Suppose you start from here and travel towards the sun in a straight line. From here the sun looks small. Suppose you go forward a million miles; it will surely seem much larger. At every stage it will become bigger and bigger. Suppose that twenty thousand photographs are taken of the same sun, all from different standpoints; these twenty thousand photographs will all certainly differ from one another. But can you deny that each is a photograph of the same sun? So all forms of religion, high or low, are just different stages in the upward journey towards the eternal Light, which is God Himself. Some embody a lower view, some a higher, and that is all the difference.

—Vivekananda, Inspired Talks 194

Even though harmlessly enough expressed, this relativistic view of truth is dangerous because it represents an assault on truth. It denies to spiritual and moral truths an absolute value by asserting that all spiritual and moral positions, no matter how contradictory they may seem, are really complementary and reconcilable because they are all less or more mature—that is, less or more evolved—readings of the same Truth. Armed with this assumption, the New-Age Movement has become just one more modern movement on the side of lawlessness and selfishness. Taking refuge in its humbug, its proselytes congratulate themselves for having found the Ancient Wisdom, the Secret of the Ages, while they construct their towers of Babel. The rest of us, if we are wise, can only brace ourselves against the coming anarchy, the confusion of tongues.

At this point, astute yoga-Vedantins will assert that I am oversimplifying their stance on morality, confusing the philosophical with the practical. Surely, they will say, one must admit that the people of India and the followers of yoga-Vedanta are among the most moral in the world. They have their Laws of Manu, their detailed instructions on the rules of *dharma* (the performance of one's duty according to his station in life), and their spiritual disciplines that emphasize purity, compassion, nonviolence, and so on. Even Swami Vivekananda's guru, Sri Ramakrishna, when speaking of transcending the dualities of life, said that the spiritual seeker must remove the thorn of ignorance (darkness, vice, evil) from his flesh with the thorn of knowledge (light, virtue, good) before he can throw them both away (M. 288). To yoga-Vedantins, then, goodness matters. Virtuous living helps propel them toward God.

But how can they so glibly distinguish between the practical and the philosophical applications? If philosophically speaking our conception of everything in the universe, including morality, is maya, a mere illusion borne of our ignorance of our true divine nature, then surely what we consider to be good and evil must be relative, as Swami Vivekananda above informs us. And this relativity must be not only ultimate but practical and temporal. Maya is that which is and isn't; therefore, good and evil are real and unreal at the same time. As Emerson put it, "Good and bad are but names very readily transferable to that or this . . ." (150).

That being the case, our concept of good will vary according to our circumstances, and our commitment to it will vary according to our tastes. What is good today may be bad tomorrow, and vice versa. What, then, becomes of morality, especially in the West where we have depended upon God-given absolutes and have never adhered to strict Eastern caste rules or social roles (*varnas*)? We must depend, like Emerson and his ilk, on our own subjective interpretations of good and evil in determining appropriate and inappropriate behavior. For this reason, many in the West today are champions of moral relativism, the offspring of Western subjectivism and Eastern monistic Vedanta. These ideological parents have formed strange hybrids in the soil of the pluralistic West. Thus in our day rationalizations for immoral behavior abound. Eastern philosophy bears much of the responsibility for this state of affairs, as I shall demonstrate in the remaining pages of this chapter.

Theological Relativism

"*Ekam sat vipra bahuda vadanti*," declares one verse in *The Upanishads*. "As many faiths, so many paths," my guru, Swami S., used to say by way of translation, lending authority at the same time to the words of Ramakrishna: "All religions are true" (M. 111). "There is but one real Occult Philosophy, and we find it in evidence everywhere—once the Truth is grasped, it is found to be the Master Key with which to unlock the various doors leading to the esoteric phase of any and all religions and philosophies," asserts a Western occultist (Ramacharaka 247-48). In other words, according to New-Age theologians, if a person has the "right" kind of knowledge or *gnosis*, he must perforce perceive that for the earnest seeker, any path to God will work.

Therefore, according to this view, differing—even contradictory—truths are all true because they all point in a single direction. The Hindu believes that God created the universe out of himself, just as a spider spins its web out of its own body. From this belief arise many distinctive assumptions and conclusions, as we have seen, about the nature of God, the universe, and man. On the other hand, the Christian believes that God created the universe out of nothing—*ex nihilo*. Likewise, from this belief arise distinctive assumptions and conclusions about the nature of God, the universe, and man.

But to the yoga-Vedantin or advanced occultist, all of these assumptions and conclusions, Hindu or Christian, are true— that is, *relatively* true. Some truths, of course, are "higher" than others, closer to the sun of truth. As long as one is seeking God, however, all of them are true—although partial and imperfect—readings of God. To these thinkers, then, the compasses of all sincere seekers are pointed in the same direction—toward God.

Ultimately, however, such truths, they admit, aren't *absolutely true* because God, the Absolute, alone is true. Everything short of God, therefore, is only relatively true, depending on the seeker's inclinations, aptitudes, desires, and fitness. For this reason, the advanced spiritual seeker isn't supposed to criticize or disturb another's faith. The Shaivite must worship his Shiva and Shakti and strive to master his body and mind through his *tantric* practices; the Christian must worship Christ and strive to spread the Good News the world over. Each religion, according to this New-Age view, has its mission and purpose, and each attracts to itself those who, by virtue of their natures or karmas, belong to its flock. In fact, "All the different religions," claims Swami Vivekananda, "are but applications of the one Religion, adapted to suit the requirements of different nations" (*Inspired Talks* 136). Fools and hypocrites, of course, will miss or distort the truth in any religion, but the sincere will always love God alone and strive for true holiness. In this respect, all worshipers worship the same God, the Absolute, who transcends time-space, matter, energy, and mind. Or so runs the argument.

This ability to perceive that all paths lead to God and then to overlook real differences between religious philosophies results in two grave problems. First, it encourages people to invent their own religious philosophies or "paths"—or, better, to adhere to no single one—because obviously any syncretistic combination works in this new age of pluralism and toleration, individualism and do-it-yourself enlightenment. The resulting confusion of tongues can only lead to a breakdown in logical discourse and meaningful communication among people within the same culture.

Consider, for example, a television broadcast by a leading New-Age prophet, Elizabeth Clare Prophet, which aired on a local public access channel in Sacramento, California, on June

114 EMBRACED BY THE DARKNESS

24, 1988, entitled "The Coming Revolution in Higher Consciousness." In no less than thirty minutes, she had spun out in her droning voice her "truths," making several references to different religious traditions and occult theories: "Buddha's renunciation and path," "silver cord," "chakras," "Christ consciousness," "I AM presence," "anointed one of God," "divine mother," "sponsorship of St. Germaine," "Judgment Day," "Vatican II," "seven rays," "highest octave," "Christ, the vine," "rebellion of Satan," "astral plane," "Krishna/Arjuna," and "the lost teachings of Jesus."

How is any rational person to make sense of such gibberish? If the speaker wriggles this way and that, if she can never be pinned down, then how can her audience draw any reasonable conclusions from her spiritual babble? Perhaps they don't want to. Perhaps they just want to feel good, as the camera seemed to prove as it panned the audience. All looked prosperous and calm; some looked positively euphoric. With such an approach to spiritual life, rational thought and discourse must surely break down because inconsistency will invariably be tolerated. How can one reconcile the "sponsorship of St. Germaine" and a faith in "Christ, the vine"? Who is the master in this case? How also can one accept the real existence of a fallen Satan, who can lure one to eternal perdition, and a "Christ consciousness" that everyone will one day attain after innumerable births? Indeed, how can one adhere to "the lost teachings of Jesus"—especially since no one, to date, has verified that they even exist—and at the same time hearken to "Buddha's renunciation and path"? It's all a muddle. A refusal of reason rules.

Second, this ability to level all religions, perceiving "unity in diversity," and to blur distinctions leads to an even more serious problem. It must surely vitiate the Christian faith as it has come down to us through the Bible and ecclesiastical tradition, for Christianity is based on the historical uniqueness, preeminence, and salvific power of Christ and his Gospel. But New-Age relativism holds that all paths are equal to Christianity in effectiveness. As long as a person believes that he holds within himself the "Master Key" to all occult knowledge, he is free to accept or reject any teaching according to his own tastes and inclinations. For him the Christian message would become just one more selection on a spiritual salad bar. A Christianity thus degraded—indeed, gutted—would gradually lose its motive force, its convictions, its faith and hope. Who, after all, would be willing to die for truths that are only relatively true? Churches across our nation and missions across the world would be as empty and silent as tombs. "What good news?" people would ask. "God is already within us and all things. All we have to do is turn within and find the truth for ourselves in the only *real* temple, the temple of our own bodies."

As a result, we will one day have transcended the need for any single religion. In every home there will be an altar on which the picture of Christ will appear with Buddha and/or Krishna, St. Germaine, Rajneesh, perhaps even, God forbid, another David Koresh. Men and women will become laws unto themselves because they will believe that God is already within them, accessible, malleable, serviceable. Emotion, not reason, will prevail. New-Age theology will have triumphed. Bhagwan Shree Rajneesh expresses this New-Age spirit perfectly:

> Listen! The Kingdom is within you! Then all temples become useless, because you are the temple. Then you are the church! Then the Vatican becomes useless, then Rome [Jerusalem also?] is just a burden. Then there is no need for Mecca and Medina, no need for a Girnar or Kashi. *You are the temple*, the live temple of God! He is within you. Then what is the need of a priest, a mediator?
>
> —*308*

Indeed, then, if we follow this logic, why would we need Christianity? Why would we need a single savior—namely, Jesus Christ? In the end, if we follow the New-Age path that is laid out for us, we will one day have the perfect generic religion, a kind of fuzzy, feel-good non-religion. Then we can all join hands, swaying, singing, with eyes closed, "We are the world; we are the children," eagerly awaiting the coming of that evolutionary moment in history when "Christs will be born in number like bunches of grapes on a vine" (Vivekananda, *Inspired Talks* 25).

Ethical Relativism

New-Agers hedge on the issue of moral absolutes, but as a rule they disclaim them. They extol the virtues of goodness and love but define and apply them in rather loose ways, advancing glittering generalities but avoiding the nitty-gritty dilemmas of daily living. After all, if they were to adhere to specific, consistent moral absolutes, they would have to hold themselves and others accountable for their actions; they would have to judge themselves and others according to set standards; they would then have to experience guilt and practice repentance. Heaven forbid! They might even have to give up their precious freedom to do as they please when they discover that the dictates of their own Higher Power or True Self are often suspect. Thus would end the preeminent rule of subjectivism.

Notice what Swami Vivekananda, the eminent Hindu philosopher, asserts about the possibility of discovering and adhering to absolute values:

> Two ways are left open to us: the way of the ignorant, who think that there is only one way to truth and that all the rest are wrong; and the way of the wise, who admit that, according to our mental constitution or the different circumstances in which we dwell, duty and morality may vary. The important thing is to know that there are gradations of duty and of morality.
>
> —*Karma-Yoga and Bhakti-Yoga* 14

The "ignorant," those of us who believe in absolutes, of course, are dismissed as inflexible bigots. Relativists must always buttress their case by first turning their opposition into straw men, mere scarecrows, and then setting them ablaze. Then they point to the obvious—every individual is unique, possessing his own mental constitution and facing his own set of circum-stances—so they can leap, like lemmings, to a daring *non sequitur*: for the individual, subjective authority must be the only ultimate authority.

To bolster their own authority to make such pronouncements, they then have to remind us that there are "gradations" of understanding, their view naturally being the highest and the ignoramuses' view being the lowest—well, maybe not the low-est, but lower. A page later in the same book, Vivekananda underscores the importance of such subjectivity by offering us a reassuring rule of thumb: "to advance we must have faith in our-selves first and then in God. He who has no faith in himself can never have faith in God. Therefore the only alternative remain-ing to us is to recognize that duty and morality vary under dif-ferent circumstances" (15). The swami's message is clear: if we believe in ourselves first, everything else will turn out just fine.

According to this view, judgment must also disappear. As the swami says a few pages later:

> Not all the men and women in any society are of the same mind, capacity, or power to do things; they must have dif-ferent ideals [later he uses the word "standard"] and we have no right to sneer at any ideal. Let everyone do the best he can to realize his own ideal. Nor is it right that I should be judged by your standard or you by mine.
>
> —*19*

Whether or not the swami recognized the implications of his words when he wrote them, his message is clear enough in the context of our modern world: you and I are free to do our own thing, as long as we don't hurt—or judge!—anyone else. What is your ideal? A million dollars in the bank and a mansion on a hill? Free love? Homosexual love? Daily communion with channeled spirits? Shamanism? Worship of the Gaia? "Hey," say the modern New-Age relativists, "that's cool." In this way, almost any "ideal" or "lifestyle" can be rationalized as one's own "spiritual path."

But curiously, after saying that morality is relative, the swami then makes absolute pronouncements: "The great duty of the householder is to earn a living, but he must take care that he does not do it by telling lies or by cheating or by robbing others; and he must remember that his life is for the service of God and the poor" (21). Even more emphatically he declares, "A householder who does not struggle to get wealth is immoral" (24). Didn't the swami just argue that no one has a right to judge another because people have different mental constitutions, capacities, powers, and circumstances? What are we to make of such foolish inconsistency? Apparently only "the wise" among us can tell. "Our duty," says the swami, addressing the most advanced subjectivists, "is to encourage everyone in his struggle to live up to his own highest ideal, and strive at the same time to make that ideal as near as possible to the truth" (19).

Here the swami returns full circle to a standard New-Age abstraction: "the truth." And yet his use of the word "truth" is equivocal. If he is referring to Absolute Truth, how can we live in conformity with it, a mere abstraction that transcends life and mind and decision-making? If he is referring to some lesser truth by which we can guide our actions, he is contradicting himself since, according to him, any truth short of Absolute Truth is merely relative. But the unwary among us have already been lulled into a false sense of security. "Ah, yes, of course, the truth," we are supposed to murmur, nodding our heads and knitting our brows. But for all our nodding and knitting, we are no closer to the truth, no matter how long we may sit at the feet of the most brilliant New-Age teacher.

If we were to examine ethical relativism within the context of social interactions, we would begin to see that it forms one link in a deadly causal chain that begins in arrogant self-sufficiency and ends in social disorder. First, the relativist, cut loose from traditional biblical morality, begins to select and assert his own values. He perceives himself to be more enlightened than others. According to Aldous Huxley in his essay "Pascal," such a person "is unlike the general run of thinkers, who are very reluctant to admit diversity, and, if they do confess the fact, deplore it." These poor souls, continues Huxley, "practice and demand consistency through fear of inconsistency, through fear of being dangerously free, through fear of life. For morality is always the product of terror; its chains and strait-waistcoats are fashioned by those who dare not trust others, because they dare not trust themselves, to walk in liberty" (*Collected Essays* 357). The liberated "life worshipper" or relativist, on the other hand, is free to "go with the flow," to reject traditional morality and welcome all new experiences. He becomes, in short, a law unto himself.

Once he is gripped by such self-sufficiency, he will develop a new broad-minded toleration and an indifference toward the traditional categories of right and wrong. As long as he is "true to himself" and "doesn't hurt anyone," he permits himself to do as he pleases. He also permits others to do the same—he allows them their own "space." He will, of course, have his causes, the popular, liberal ones, the "politically correct" ones sanctioned by all the other relativists: animal rights, gay rights, abortion rights. For to the relativist, everyone has a "right" to do his own thing. But he will avoid making judgments about others "who are doing their own thing" because to do so would be to admit that there might be some moral absolutes rather than just personal or cultural preferences. After all, he will tell you, in some cultures the people practice polygamy, whereas in our culture we practice monogamy. It's all relative, you know.

In his quest for self-fulfillment, then, armed with glib rationalizations, he will violate hitherto inviolable moral laws and excuse the sins of others. In so doing, he will sear his conscience and lose the capacity to examine himself in light of God's laws and repent of his moral lapses, all in the name of "spiritual evolution" and "social progress." And all the while he will exult in his independence and inconsistency.

Where both the individual and society are concerned, this stubborn self-sufficiency and indifference to traditional notions of right and wrong can only have one ultimate result: confusion. When right is called wrong and wrong right, one can rationalize almost any course of action. When I was involved with New-Age Christians in the early 1970s, I witnessed this rationalized relativism in action. In the name of "love" and "forgiveness of self," many of these people were able to violate traditional sexual mores. A "healing session," for example, might lead a New-Age counselor to engage in sexual therapy with a married woman, who was already so confused that she could mistake his overtures for love and later forgive herself, affirming that her need for love had been met. I knew two older married women who carried this "love" a step farther: they engaged in a one-night sexual triangle with a young unmarried man. Even though one of them was old enough to be the young man's mother, she saw nothing amiss in her "loving" behavior. In fact, she told me she believed that even Jesus himself had sex with Mary Magdalene in an effort to purify and heal her. In this case and in many others we encounter today, liberty quickly degenerates into license, and license into licentiousness.

Eventually, once such conduct becomes permissible, even "normal," traditional institutions—marriage, family, and the like—must disintegrate, leaving whole groups of people broken and bewildered. Evidence of this growing chaos is all around us today. Premarital sex is commonplace. Men and women move into and out of each other's apartments almost as quickly as an avocado can ripen and rot. Children are sexually abused. At alarming rates young people are dropping out of high schools or committing suicide before they can even receive their diplomas. People of all social classes, it seems, abuse drugs. Hyped up, hopped up, irresponsible teenagers join gangs or go "wilding" in Central Park or spray a playground with bullets, hoping to drop a rival to his knees. Although the rest of us traditionalists cry out, the political pundits and spiritual gurus refuse to listen. They simply continue to assault us with their psychobabble about "self-actualization," "self-esteem," "values clarification," "environmental conditioning," and "situational ethics."

Of course, high-minded New-Agers would be appalled by my accusation that they are fueling the fires of moral confusion and social disorder. None of them would condone rape, murder, heroin addiction, or child abuse. Yet herein lies their inconsistency. Apparently they are willing to draw lines, but they won't explain where or why those lines are to be drawn. True, they will affirm a general principle: renounce anything that separates you from God. But such a guiding principle is inadequate. It ignores the real world in which we all must live, work, and make difficult, specific moral decisions that involve everyone around us. It allows us to trust a subjective feeling and deny that any objective truths exist. To the high-minded seer, objective reality is too complex and messy, but subjective "truth" is oh-so-clear. Yet as we have found, feeling good about an action isn't proof that we are progressing toward God and operating according to his will.

If New-Agers possessed any integrity, they would at the very least accept as a criterion of right Kant's categorical imperative. Then they would at least say, "I would want this action universalized (namely, taken up by everyone), or I wouldn't want this action universalized." But even this definition of right is too hard for them because they would be forced to extend their thinking

122 \ EMBRACED BY THE DARKNESS

beyond themselves, beyond their preoccupation with their own "liberation." They would have to consider the implications of their decisions in light of the common human welfare and the short-term as well as long-range effects of such behavior on others. And, of course, because of their underlying faith in subjectivism and relativism, they can't.

THE ANTIDOTE: CHRISTIAN ABSOLUTISM

Fortunately, moral absolutes, as our Judeo-Christian tradition asserts, do exist. Some actions are absolutely wrong, some, absolutely right. Any other conclusion is absurd. Who, for example, but a monster or an intellectual zombie could argue that the sexual abuse of a three-year-old child is ever conceivably right, based on the circumstances and the inclinations of the persons involved? Who could ever, under any circumstances, condone the mugging and beating of an innocent old woman in her own home or the raping of a jogger in Central Park? Who but a brutal Nazi could see goodness in genocide? Once we concede that there is even one absolute, we must entertain the possibility that there are others; and to do so, we must appeal to some authority for our standards. In today's world every right-thinking person should consider it his duty to seek out these absolute standards, because the very survival of the human race depends upon our identification of and adherence to them.

Similarly, if there are moral absolutes, then there must be spiritual absolutes—that is, right and wrong ways by which we may understand, please, and honor God. And these spiritual absolutes needn't merely be generalized ones that please as many and offend as few as possible—for example, we should love God with all our hearts, minds, souls, and strength and our neighbors as ourselves. Even yoga-Vedantins will accede to the general truths. We must have the integrity to seek out the particular truths and the moral courage to affirm and obey them.

But in doing so, we will have to take a stand. Because as Christians we regard Jesus' pronouncements as absolutes, we must affirm even those sayings that don't support the popular New-Age notion of "unity in diversity." Consider "I am the way and the truth and the life. No one comes to the Father except through me" (John 14:6). If we accept this assertion as merely relatively true, we will have to deny Christ's exclusive claim to Sonship and scuttle Christianity, for to deny that Christ is the only redeemer is not only to say that Christ is a liar but to say that there are other redeemers, and if there are other redeemers, then there are other paths to redemption, including the path of self-effort. If, on the other hand, we accept Christ's assertion about himself as absolutely true, we will have to affirm Christ's Sonship and face the persecution that follows from such an affirmation.

For any of this appeal to moral and spiritual absolutes to make sense, we must understand that they have but one source, one authority—God, who reveals them objectively to us through his Word, and most especially his Word in action, his Son. True, he may sometimes reveal them to us through reason or spiritual traditions. But he *always* reveals them to us through the Bible, the ever trustworthy, inerrant, authoritative Word of God. He speaks through the prophets and the history of his people in the Old Testament, and he speaks through the life, works, and words of Jesus and his apostles in the New Testament. And once we have accepted Jesus as our Savior, he speaks to our hearts by means of the Holy Spirit. But always, to paraphrase Martin Luther, our consciences must remain captive to the Word of God if we are to live rightly. To seek out "new" moral and spiritual truths from other sources is to fall back on exclusively human resources and to end up once again in the camp of the New-Agers, exalting human subjectivity and proclaiming the high holiness of relativism.

Even now certain readers will be revolting against the apparent dogmatism in the preceding paragraph. But before they read on, I urge them to consider this thought: the appeal of relativism is precisely that it allows us to do, be, think, or imagine anything we want, free of external constraints. It's easy to be a relativist. Absolutism, on the other hand, is hard because it requires obedience and self-sacrifice, neither of which is popular with our selfish natures or in this selfish age. Orthodox Christianity, then, must seem cold, uncreative, and inflexible to our human nature because we would rather be sailing along in our own way at our own speed, unhampered by any absolute authority or impositions from outside ourselves. Whenever the rules are spelled out, we are naturally going to rebel against them because it's in our natures to do so. Clearly, however, it's our duty to resist our natures when we can see that our unchecked, unexamined actions will produce evil.

Let those who object to my absolutism consider this thought also: if as a society we continue to race along our current path, toward greater and greater manifestations of subjectivism and relativism, we will find ourselves becoming ever more desensitized toward the real presence of evil around us. Like the yoga-Vedantins, we will call it "illusion," denying its power altogether; or like the occultists, we will ignore it; or like the secular humanists, we will excuse it by blaming it on poverty or negligent parents or particles in the ozone. Such philosophies continue to promote relativism, directly or indirectly, because they refuse to deal with real evil in the world. And yet as our modern era has proven to those of us who still adhere to traditional values, evil flourishes when "truth" and "goodness" become relative terms and when evil isn't defined, recognized, and battled for what it is: a rank sickness in the hearts of men.

Therefore, if we don't begin to acknowledge our desperate need for absolutes, we will continue to pay, I fear, a terrible price for our maximal freedom and minimal responsibility. And untold numbers of souls, good relativists all, will become insensible to the message of salvation by grace through faith, for they won't understand that there is a Moral Law that *can* be broken, a Moral Law that they themselves have broken again and again. Thus unrepentant, they won't be able to grasp that the only way to unconditional forgiveness and divine reconciliation is through Jesus Christ. More and more people, with a shrug of their shoulders, will simply say, "What! Me a sinner? I've followed my heart in all matters. Man, you're not making any sense. I'm okay and you're okay—just the way we are. Everything is relative."

6

A BOUQUET OF WITHERED
REINCARNATIONS

URING A PAST-LIFE READING IN 1971 A "SPIRIT GUIDE"
speaking through a trance medium—a man with a bona
fide doctoral degree—told me that I had been a swami in my last
life. "Your name," he said, expertly rolling his *r*, "was Guran-
anda." It was only five years later, after I had studied Sanskrit,
that I learned that it's grammatically impossible to join *guru*
with *ananda* by dropping the *u* at the end of *guru*. Words that
are joined to *ananda* in this way must end with a long *a*.
Although some people might attribute the learnéd medium's
error to a slip of the tongue, I concluded, even long before I
stopped believing in reincarnation, that his past-life reading was
a sham.

But this medium wasn't the only psychic to regale me with his
vivid and imaginative insights. According to one, my soul was no
more than 30,000 years old; according to another, my soul was
4,700,000 years old. At various other times, still other psychics
told me that I had been an American Indian, a troubadour, an
Elizabethan actor, and a medieval monk who had been beaten
mercilessly with chains and clubs (a brutal act that was supposed
to explain why my spine is crooked). On my own I "discovered"
that I had been a sixteenth-century Dutch printer and book-
binder, a nineteenth-century barrister, and a G.I. who had died

during World War II. This latter life I "knew" to be true because in the mid-1950s—like millions of other male baby boomers—I had enjoyed playing with polyethylene army men and watching John Wayne and Audie Murphy in World War II movies.

None of these "revelations," however, ever brought me the spiritual wisdom, peace, and joy that I so much craved and that they were supposed to deliver. They were, however, fascinating and titillating. Like any other diversion, they occupied hours of my waking thoughts. But they never helped me put my "present-life problems" into perspective, nor did they enable me to understand my "karmic ties" and "lessons." In fact, in the end the excitement they produced turned into restlessness and discontent, not because I was immoderate in my pursuit of spiritual truth, but because the "past lives" had provided me with no *certain* knowledge. I became self-absorbed and preoccupied but not illumined or wise, unless the fact that I became wise in my own conceit may redound to my credit.

Therefore, my past-life revelations had no value, except perhaps that they afforded me a temporary escape, like a novel or movie, from anxiety and self-doubt. Like many past-life seekers, I remained dissatisfied with and uneasy about my past-life experiences, haunted by the eerie sensation that I was merely deluding myself. In the pit of my stomach I felt that something was terribly wrong, even while the "answers" provided by the theory of reincarnation seemed so right.

Despite the weirdness, hysteria, humbug, and narcissism that seem to attend an individual's search for past lives, the acceptance of reincarnation plays an integral part in a seeker's conversion to New-Age theology. Many New-Age seekers, in fact, come to the New-Age Movement by way of a belief in reincarnation alone. In my own case, I came to believe in reincarnation at an early age because my father and my grandmother, a simple woman who knew nothing about Western Occultism or yoga-Vedanta, believed in it. Naturally, then, when I first began to hunger for

God, my belief in reincarnation limited and directed my search, carrying me away from orthodox Christianity. In most cases today, however, people simply come to believe because reincarnationist ideas are "in the air." Indeed, our airwaves fairly bristle with these ideas. Not long ago, for example, *Unsolved Mysteries* ran a long segment about a young man who experienced a detailed past-life recall during which he "remembered" that he had died during World War II in a submarine accident.

Millions of Americans simply come to believe in the theory because they are convinced that it makes sense. More importantly, they find the whole notion to be comforting. To their human natures, it seems not only benign but divine. And yet as a fundamental tenet of New-Age theology, reincarnation carries with it all the dangerous assumptions about God, the universe, and man that I have already exposed in the previous chapters. For this reason, because by itself the belief in reincarnation so effectively pushes people away from Christ and Christian truth, the arguments for and against it deserve to be examined in a special chapter.

Over the years reincarnationists have advanced many arguments in favor of their theory. Mostly they have appealed purely to the authority of subjective experience by relating their "spiritual" insights. The Hindu scriptures and the writings of Theosophists, Rosicrucians, and many other occultists testify to this approach. Sometimes they have even tried to use the Bible itself to support their position by referring to passages in the New Testament—John 3:3, John 9:1-2, Matthew 11:13-14, and so on. Reason is sufficient to refute the subjective arguments, and only a little contextual exegesis is required to refute the arguments that rely on scriptural passages (see Morey, *Reincarnation* 33-35; Albrecht 35-41). For this reason, I will examine only those arguments for reincarnation that appeal to three main areas of authority: science, psychology, and ethics.

REINCARNATION: THE SCIENTIFIC ARGUMENT

As most of us know, modern materialistic science has to a great extent undermined people's faith in Christian theology and tradition. Reincarnationists have taken advantage of this doubt by aligning themselves with modern science. They even claim that the ancient wisdom has been vindicated by modern science: modern scientific truths now confirm the ancient occultic truths about the nature of man and the universe. In this way, by associating themselves with science and also relying on pseudo-scientific terminology, they have managed to make their theory sound all the more plausible. However, their assumptions and conclusions remain as unscientific as they have always been.

The Reincarnationist's First Scientific Argument

Proof positive exists that we have lived before, reincarnationists claim. Consider the countless stories of people like Bridey Murphy, the young man who was profiled on *Unsolved Mysteries*, and others. Examine the many cases compiled by Dr. Ian Stevenson in his book *Twenty Cases for Reincarnation*. Again and again researchers have investigated people's stories and painstakingly investigated the facts. In many of these cases of past-life recall, they have been able to prove that the present-life person and the past-life person are one and the same. Scientific proof is thus irrefutably established.

The Christian Objection and Refutation

There are other explanations for these phenomena. Such "evidence" merely *seems* to support the conclusion that reincarnation is true.

The first objection is by now a cliché. The person who related his past life either knew of the person whose life he related or knew enough about the historical setting to make the story plausible in most of its details. I won't offend the intelligence and goodwill of reincarnationists by pursuing this obvious objection. When subjects have wittingly or unwittingly fabricated their past-life memories by drawing on their present-life knowledge or experience, reincarnationists have been capable of admitting so.

The second objection, however, is perfectly fair and reasonable. Because reincarnationists believe that ESP or psychic intuitions exist, the objection can be stated simply: the person who claims to be recalling his past life may in fact be simply "tuning in" either to someone who did exist in the past or to sets of general details that applied to several people who existed in the past. If the air or the "ethers" are alive, as New-Agers claim, with the thoughts of others, both living and dead, then sensitive souls should be able to gain access to these thoughts or presences. Because New-Agers have used the analogy of radio or TV waves when explaining ESP, they should have no trouble in conceding that this theory of attunement by itself could explain all instances of past-life recall.

The third objection is the most provocative of the three. It's therefore the one that is most likely to offend reincarnationists. Because they admit to the existence of a spiritual world and the presence of "mischievous," if not evil, spirits in that world, this argument can also be simply stated: cases of recall may merely prove that evil spirits can and do deceive unwary mortals. Being incorporeal, these spirits have access to knowledge that humans lack. Such evil spirits, if Christians are correct, willfully and maliciously set out, by whatever means, to estrange us from God, even using the name of God. And they may do so, as Paul tells us, as angels of light—that is, as apparent bearers of truth and light. Hence, the ability of experiences of past lives to dazzle and uplift us doesn't prove they are true. Our subjective responses prove nothing, except that a variety of experiences, good or bad, true or false, can make us *feel* good.

The theory of reincarnation, then, isn't the only answer in

cases of apparent recall. In logic a truth is only self-evident if only one answer to the same question is possible. For example, to the question "Is there such an object as a round square?" there is only one answer: "No." The answer is self-evident because it's impossible to assert that there *is* such an object as a round square. Thus, on the question of reincarnation, scientific proof isn't established; more than one explanation of the phenomena is possible.

The Reincarnationist's Second Scientific Argument

Moreover, claim the proponents of reincarnation, the theory of reincarnation is based on an understanding of spiritual evolution that corresponds to the scientific understanding of evolution. The reincarnationist view is logically compatible with the scientific view. As the soul encounters one experience after another while incarnated in the material world, it gradually attains to higher and higher levels of consciousness as it learns its karmically dictated lessons. Thus it drops and takes up form after form as it rises on the scale of evolution from the blood cell to the enlightened master, step by step, according to its awareness of the truth and to the intensity of its efforts.

The Christian Objection and Refutation

The term "evolution" as it's used by reincarnationists, however, isn't scientific at all, for they have failed to consider the two main factors involved in evolution: natural selection and sexual selection. According to evolutionists, creatures evolve because they adapt to changes in their environments, without regard to any *moral* purpose or design. If the temperature drops thirty degrees, over time certain members of a species develop heavier body hair. Among these, it's the sexually attractive and fit who breed and survive. The attainment of "higher levels of consciousness," therefore, has nothing to do with evolution as it's scientifically understood. In a struggle for survival in a technologically sophisticated world, it may well be the most brutal and callous who survive, not the harbingers of pacifism, meditation, and holism.

Likewise, even if evolutionists were to grant the existence of a human soul, there is no scientific basis for the belief that there is an infallible, absolute law of karma that regulates the affairs of men and the passage of their souls from one body to another. Any law that would guarantee that a soul is rewarded from life to life according to its moral and spiritual merits would have to be, at least in part, supernatural and transcendental. Yet the theory of evolution doesn't—and can't by virtue of its scientific basis—recognize supernatural moral laws. According to evolutionists, in fact, moral laws are natural and man-made—they are products of man's evolution.

"[T]he moral sense," says Darwin in the "General Summary and Conclusion" of his *Descent of Man*, "follows, firstly, from the enduring and ever present nature of the social instincts; secondly, from man's appreciation of the approbation and disapprobation of his fellows; and thirdly, from the high activity of his mental faculties, with past impressions extremely vivid" (592). One paragraph later Darwin goes on to say, "As all men desire their own happiness, praise or blame is bestowed on actions and motives, according as they lead to this end; and as happiness is an essential part of the general good, the greatest-happiness principle indirectly serves as a nearly safe standard of right and wrong" (592). In this way, according to the theory of evolution, men—in their efforts to survive, find happiness, and enjoy one another's approval—devise and obey their own evolving moral laws. Therefore, from a purely scientific point of view, no one can prove that a supernatural law of karma exists.

Finally, reincarnationists must explain why we can find no empirical evidence to support their contention that a law of spiritual evolution is operating in the material world. Population growth, they claim, does provide such evidence. The population of the world has been increasing rather than decreasing, they tell us, because souls from the animal kingdom have been moving up into the human kingdom. But if, simultaneously, advanced souls in the human kingdom are also being liberated, why would the rate of population growth increase so rapidly? Why wouldn't the size of the world's population stabilize to a certain extent since at every moment some souls are entering and some exiting the human race? Evolution, one would have to conclude, operates faster for animals, who lack willpower and reason, than it does for humans, who possess willpower and reason. So old Socrates is still laboring on, body after body, while Jojo the circus chimp suddenly acquires a human body and learns to use a computer. Animals by the millions rush into human forms, while humans remain stuck as humans for millennia.

And why, the reincarnationists must tell us, would so many animals be suddenly joining the human race? Have humans been treating animals so well that the animals, now wiser, are ready for human births? How could this be? From an animal-rights point of view, a distinctly New-Age position, we still exploit animals as much as, if not more than, we ever did before. For our own purposes we vivisect, exterminate, and consume them. Is their mere contact with us, positive or negative, making them evolve more rapidly (even as they pass through our stomachs, as one of my New-Age friends used to argue)? If such is the case, would reincarnationists then argue that all the escalating violence perpetrated today by humans against humans is a form of retribution? Animals, no longer animals but now unevolved humans, are maiming and killing their former human tormentors. Given the segments of the population who now commit most violent crimes, any widespread acceptance of this hypothesis would surely only promote more classism, sexism, and racism in a world already riven by hate and violence. Such thinking is preposterous and inhumane. In no way does population growth provide evidence for a theory of "spiritual evolution."

Let reincarnationists also explain why spiritual evolution isn't producing a better, safer world. If over aeons many souls have had the opportunity to evolve spiritually, we would expect to find today many enlightened souls, many masters, dwelling among us. We would further expect that these compassionate souls, with their ability to master themselves and nature, would be able to assume positions of leadership in the world and bring peace and prosperity to their nations, joining with other masters to do the same for the world. Even if they decided to become spiritual rather than secular leaders, we would expect the sum total of wisdom in the world to be on the increase. We might expect also to witness miracles. With so much suffering in the world, these masters would surely be making themselves known in every nation, healing the sick, raising the dead, leading the way.

But they aren't appearing. The world is just as barbaric and benighted—perhaps even more so—than it ever was before. Technology has not brought us peace, nor have political and economic systems founded on "enlightened" principles. Everywhere we can still witness man's inhumanity to man. And far from merely hearing today a still, sad music of humanity, we hear instead a shrill, mad music of inhumanity blaring out of boom boxes, issuing up from our city streets, invading our homes via satellites, encroaching on our lives.

Thus science doesn't support the theory of reincarnation. In fact, in light of the observations and methods of science, it's more logical to conclude that there is nothing after death than to believe that future human births and a regulatory law of spiritual evolution exist. Let reincarnationists, therefore, renounce their pseudo-scientific efforts to convince us.

REINCARNATION: THE PSYCHOLOGICAL ANSWER

Using modern psychology with its belief in a conscious and subconscious mind, reincarnationists have tried to explain why a person may be attracted to one object but repelled by another or why he may take one course of action rather than another. Hidden tendencies from past lives, they claim, lie buried in the subconscious, ready to manifest when stimulated by certain circumstances. No person, therefore, is born into his present life with a *tabula rasa*, a clean slate. Even a newborn infant contains within him the multitudinous impressions—some active, some latent—created by his experiences in his previous births. In this way, New-Agers are able to legitimize past-life regression as a therapy, placing it alongside psychotherapy as just one more tool for helping people achieve self-actualization.

The Reincarnationist's Psychological Argument

Because the theory of reincarnation best explains human psychological development, a person who explores his past lives is in the best possible position to solve present-life problems. By studying and coming to terms with past-life memories—the immediate and remote causes of his present-life thoughts and emotions—he can maximize his potential and enhance his spiritual progress.

The Christian Objection and Refutation

The reincarnationist must first explain how we can live many lives, yet not remember them in sufficient detail to verify them, especially when such memories are said to be essential to solving present-life problems. If we can't verify the various details, how can we tell whether we are remembering or merely imagining these details? Wouldn't we be foolish, then, to place our faith in these unverifiable details of "past lives"? Verifiability would seem to be essential to an earnest seeker of truth. Otherwise, like interpreters of dream symbols, we would never know whether or not we have understood the messages of truth inherent in our past-life memories. Because many interpretations would be possible, we could just as easily conclude that our "memories" are simply elaborate dreams and nothing more. The wisdom we gained, like the yoga-Vedantin's maya, could either be or not be. How could we ever know?

Reincarnationists must also explain why, even if we have the memories of our past lives buried deep within our subconscious minds, we aren't driven to the brink of confusion, if not insanity, by the force and complexity of our past-life memories. We know that the subconscious mind affects our conscious mind in untold ways, whether we recognize these effects or not. If I have lived, say, ten thousand lives, how would I ever know who I am? Which personality would really be mine? With which one should I identify, given the fact that I have probably manifested over the aeons many different gradations of consciousness? If I had been, say, Socrates, wouldn't I be better off trusting his judgment rather than my own? But in that case I wouldn't be true to myself, right? Or would I? Actually, then, if examined in this light, any recall of past lives would necessarily be destructive to the integrity of one's present personality.

The Reincarnationist's First Counterargument

True, the memories are buried deep within the subconscious mind, but they lie beneath the memories of our present life. Even though these past-life memories are within us, we remember some but not others because the memories are either too deep to retrieve or irrelevant, according to the law of karma, to our present circumstances. Besides, the conscious mind in this life isn't the same as the conscious mind from a past life; therefore, it can't identify all past-life memories as its own because of their foreignness, as when a person in this life is a woman whereas in a past life she was a man. Ultimately we remember only as much from our past lives as we need to. In this way, we aren't overwhelmed by our past-life memories. The health of the person's mind and soul is primary; the recall of verifiable details is at best secondary.

The Christian Objection and Refutation

First, it must be asked, "How are the memories stored in the subconscious mind?" If they are stored chronologically, layer upon layer, then yesterday's memory should be more vivid than last year's memory. In that case, the reincarnationist's theory of past-life recall might make sense. But such isn't the case. Sometimes a memory of ten years ago—an accident, for example—can be keener and more vivid than yesterday's lunch of fish and chips. Therefore, a memory can't be irretrievable because of its depth or distance in time.

It would seem, then, that memories are stored according to their intensity (or their significance to the individual). First, as in the case of a habit or skill, repetition and need keep the memory very much present, as when a concert pianist brings to bear on his performance all his years of training and practice. Second, as in the case of a memorable event, we may recall the experience because of the great significance we have attached to it. Moments of intense pain or joy certainly qualify here, as do extraordinary experiences. An adult, for example, who received little love as a child may remember vividly the moment when a teacher showed him kindness and affection.

Now then, if memories are essentially stored according to their intensity, we should be able to remember significant moments from past lives, whether we "need" to know them or not, for all trivial experiences are alike, in this life or so-called past lives, in that we forget them easily, and all significant experiences and repeated habits are alike in that we remember them easily. Certainly there must be nontraumatic (perhaps, for instance, triumphant) memories from past lives that rank high enough in intensity that we should be able to remember them now, particularly if such memories could help us resolve some moral dilemma we are currently facing. But, of course, we don't remember verifiable details of this kind from past lives because in fact we have no past lives.

Second, the conscious mind in this life, to be sure, wouldn't be the same as the conscious mind in a past life, but the subconscious mind has no barriers or divisions in it. If it did, then we couldn't tap, as New-Agers claim we can, into our "unlimited subconscious potential," for this potential would then be compartmentalized and hence inaccessible. Likewise, if we couldn't remember some past-life experiences because our past minds were unlike our present mind, then we wouldn't be able to remember any past-life experiences. Our various minds, being different and mutually exclusive in form and content, wouldn't allow for any interchange between them, just as two mutually exclusive categories may not overlap, as in the case of puppy love and oxygen masks. But clearly past minds and the present mind must be similar because they belong to the same category— namely, mind—and they are constituted of the same elements— namely, thoughts. Therefore, there is no reason why any of us shouldn't remember past-life experiences spontaneously, whether we believe they exist or not or want to access them or not. But again, we don't remember them because in fact they don't exist.

Finally, if our present problems, dilemmas, and crises are linked to past lives and our purpose in life is to overcome these and gain wisdom, then reincarnation is cruel and arbitrary, for if the source of or key to a person's present problem is concealed from him within a past-life memory that he can't retrieve, how can he solve his present problem in a meaningful way? Is he bound to repeat the problem endlessly, stumbling in the dark, proceeding by trial and error?

"But wait," a New-Ager might declare, "a person may examine himself, quite apart from the recollection of his past lives, and make wise and appropriate decisions, ones that free him from past-life mistakes." If that is true, then I would submit that past-life memories are superfluous and argue further that reincarnationists should cease immediately to explore—or encourage others to explore—past lives, especially since so-called past lives can't be verified anyway. Will a wise man pin his hopes on the "lessons" represented by unsubstantiated phantasms?

It also won't do here to oversimplify the matter, to say that we will discover the answers from our past lives when we need to by means of some divinely ordained intuition, for in strictly human terms, it's by reason that we understand a problem (its aspects, its importance, its remote and immediate causes) and its solutions, and it's by the use of our wills that we correct the problem. Besides, if we can't remember our "past lives," then we also won't have access to an intuition of them; and even if we did have such access, that intuition would necessarily be flawed since the very problem with which we are now grappling wasn't resolved then, in our former life. The error in judgment that existed then still exists now. Hence, one can't use an appeal to intuition as an appeal to authority either.

The Reincarnationist's Second Counterargument

But memories of our past lives aren't stored in our current subconscious mind. They remain stored in the akashic records, where all past-life memories, even race memories, are stored. In this way, we may draw or receive from the akashic records only as much as we can safely handle in our present life. The law of karma will protect us.

The Christian Objection and Refutation

That memories of our past lives are stored in some nebulous, transcendental akashic records and not in our subconscious minds is illogical.

If from life to life a person is the same soul (or entity) regardless of the different forms he assumes, then he must always possess within him the sum total of all that he has been, done, and thought. By means of our senses, we experience the world around us, and then these sensations, as they enter our minds, are impressed upon our minds as memories, with varying degrees of intensity, and upon our souls as knowledge to which we must have access if we are to continue to "advance" or "evolve" spiritually. If sense experiences weren't impressed on the mind and soul in this way, we would remember nothing from this life or any others. Thus, when the soul reincarnates, according to the logic of the reincarnationists, it must carry its seminal memories (*samskaras*), as well as its acquired knowledge, with it. Reincarnationists readily admit to this idea, for none of them accepts Locke's theory that the mind is a *tabula rasa*. To New-Agers and yoga-Vedantins alike, the mind is never a blank slate when one is reborn. Clearly, then, the akashic-record concept flies in the face of not only common sense but also New-Age assumptions about spiritual evolution.

If reincarnationists were to modify their argument to read, "Some memories are stored in the subconscious and some are stored in the akashic records," a problem would still exist. If a person didn't have access to some of his memories—and hence some of his accumulated wisdom—he wouldn't necessarily be himself in a new life. The whole of anything always consists of the sum of its parts; if parts are missing, it isn't whole. The possession of some memories and not others, therefore, would violate the unity and integrity of the mind and soul—the conscious entity. The soul wouldn't be able to achieve spiritual unity and wholeness if it were denied access to parts of itself.

If, therefore, the mind or soul—or, better, the subconscious mind—contains within it all that the person has been, done, or thought, then it follows that the individual carries these memories with him from life to life. Amnesia and brain-damaged victims aside, this is sound psychology. But if millions of unremembered memories from perhaps thousands of lives were stored in the subconscious mind at any given moment, then one would surely be pressured and driven by unseen, unknown, often contradictory forces within him. What would prevent all these accumulated memories from trickling—or exploding—into his mind and confusing him? "Should I," a young man might ask himself, "become a stone mason, a teacher, a doctor, a black-smith, a witch doctor, or a female impersonator?" Bewildered by the experiences of his former personalities, he would be con-stantly asking himself, "Who am I, and what should I do?" If all memories of this kind were stored within our minds, without understanding why, most, if not all, of us would soon become insane—more than likely schizophrenic.

The notion of the akashic records, therefore, is a rationaliza-tion and fiction. First, it simply helps reincarnationists circum-vent problems associated with past-life recall. Second, as a kind of library suspended somewhere in a spiritual ether, it simply helps psychics and trance mediums explain how they can read someone else's past lives. When they close their eyes, they don't enter or study the other person's soul. They don't read his mind. They go instead to the akashic records. Such an explanation, it would seem, would be far less threatening to the superstitious and far more intriguing to the credulous.

REINCARNATION: THE ETHICAL ANSWER

It has always been difficult for the theodocïst to explain how a good God can permit evil to exist in his creation. Seizing on this doubt, reincarnationists have declared that it's not God but the law of karma that allows people to suffer, because it's the infal-lible law of karma that ensures that people receive their just deserts. For many New-Agers, this argument alone justifies their belief in reincarnation. It's also the one argument that is most likely to leave Christians tongue-tied. Of course, a Christian can argue that reincarnation is incompatible with biblical doctrines concerning the afterlife, final judgment, and resurrection. But the reincarnationist, who usually doesn't accept the authority of the Bible, is likely to remain unmoved by appeals to Scripture and tradition.

The Reincarnationist's Ethical Argument

The theory of reincarnation is more humane, claim reincarnationists, than the Christian one-life theory. Reincarnation better explains the inequities in the world—the differences in people's circumstances and abilities. Why should a child in Beverly Hills, for example, be born into wealth and live a long and prosperous life when another child in Ethiopia starves before he reaches his third birthday? Reincarnation and the law of karma assure us that our circumstances are determined according to unerring cosmic justice: as we sow, we reap; as we think, we become. According to the theory of reincarnation, each person is the maker of his own destiny and therefore has the power to alter his destiny and redeem himself.

The Christian Objection and Refutation

The theory of reincarnation is by no means more humane than the Christian one-life view because reincarnation fails to be just on three accounts.

First, because one should but doesn't remember his past lives, he must suffer for deeds of which he remains ignorant. The child starving in Ethiopia can't comprehend or rectify his mistake, whatever it happens to be; nor can anyone else who is reaping the evil fruits of karma. How can one possibly accept that his punishment fits his crime if he doesn't even know what his crime is? Not even human justice, as imperfect as it is, makes a person pay for a crime without first specifying—and making sure that he understands—the crime for which he is to be tried and punished.

Here all the reincarnationists can offer by way of a defense are two feeble explanations. First, they say, before coming into a body and after leaving it, the individual understands the reasons for his suffering. After death and before birth everything is clear. But of what benefit would such a disparity between our awareness in the spiritual world and our awareness in the material world be? If we are shrouded in ignorance while on earth, how can we possibly make any spiritual progress? Life would then seem to be nothing but a cruel joke played by God. "In the material world," he would be saying in effect, "my punishments will make you feel the sting of injustice and embitter you; in the spiritual world, my true intentions shall be revealed to you so that you can laugh at yourself as I do." But, of course, if ever this gap between our awareness in the spiritual world and in the material world were to be closed, it would also mean that we would be able to remember our past lives—and the "spiritual periods" between them—in detail, which, of course, we can't. How could one ever attain enlightenment of any kind when he is subjected to such fickleness by God and steeped in such ignorance while residing in this world?

Second, while suffering in this life, they say, a person comes to intuitively grasp the lesson that his suffering is teaching him, whether or not he understands the causes of his suffering. Again, as I argued before, this intuition must necessarily be faulty since it's rooted in the past-life problem of which he is ignorant. If, however, the reincarnationist insists that the intuition comes from God or his True Self, then reincarnation becomes superfluous again—past lives needn't exist. Once reincarnationists concede to this truth, they would then have to accept what Christians already know: we learn our spiritual lessons by understanding God and submitting to his will, not by probing our own psyches for past lives and then analyzing the highly suspect details that we may discover.

Moreover, far from explaining the inequalities of condition in the world, the theory of reincarnation only exacerbates them by denying to sufferers the compassion and help they need. One always hears reincarnationists say, "Let's not interfere with their karma." The fear here is that by meddling they will impede the working of karma and, worse, incur more bad karma for themselves. But clearly this attitude must lead to a breakdown in individual moral responsibility and must damage society as a whole.

To perceive the deleterious social effects of a widespread belief in reincarnation, one has only to study India, the country in which this belief has prevailed for centuries. Until Western civilization and thus Christianity began to have an impact on India, India had carried such "Don't touchism" to extremes, the caste system being the primary example. Without having any mitigating Christian beliefs in charity for its own sake, people who follow this doctrine maintain a *laissez-faire* attitude toward their less fortunate, benighted brothers and sisters. In fact, because reincarnationists are working out their own karma, they really don't pay much attention to others at all.

Most unjust of all, reincarnation consigns individuals to endless rounds of births and deaths, life after life of ignorance, bondage, and suffering—at least until they come to their senses. As a reincarnationist one doesn't hear the still, sad music of humanity but a shrill, wild, cacophonous cry that issues up before God. Humans are strapped to a wheel until they awaken to the "truth," after which they struggle like mad to free themselves so they can reach some vague goal—union with Brahman or some distant state of perfection. Until then, if we may take New-Agers as examples of this path, reincarnationists either seek pleasure and wealth as a means of mastering their environment or practice spiritual austerities and meditation as means of achieving wholeness, wellness, integration, oneness, or some such ill-defined "higher state of consciousness."

All of these seekers, it would seem, have one thing in common: they are trying to avoid or escape suffering. But how can they? Each time a person is reborn he has to start all over again with a new personality—enduring incompetent parents and teachers, rebelling against authority, making often-grievous mistakes, experiencing broken marriages, homes, and hearts—without even being able to grasp the causes of his present suffering. Who, then, except a hedonist, a masochist, or a fool would want to be born again into a human body? Who in his right mind would want to face the responsibilities and the risks again or think such a system just? It's sufficient that we live one life well, that we endure the considerable toils, temptations, and tribulations of one life, after which we may take our rest, if we have submitted to the rule of Jesus Christ, in the eternal kingdom of heaven.

This divinely ordained plan is indeed just, for God asks no more of us in our human lives than that, by means of his grace through faith, we love him and our neighbor and obey his will—passively by cheerfully enduring those hardships over which we have no control, actively by following in the footsteps of our Lord and Master, Jesus Christ. As for suffering and evil, they shall always remain, in some sense, a mystery, just as God, whose ways are above our own and whose reasons are beyond our ken, must always remain a mystery. "There is a mystery connected with suffering," says one Christian scholar, "that God has not been pleased to explain to His creatures in the present. It is sufficient for faith to trust implicitly in God Himself who will ultimately reveal that suffering was in some manner indispensable to the full manifestation of His glory" (Johnson 24).

Or as Luther might have put it, God's alien work (suffering) must be humbly borne so that his proper work (salvation) may be accomplished. That suffering is—and must remain—a paradox is amply proven by the crucifixion and resurrection of Christ himself. The Christian approach, then, is *not to flee* from inevitable suffering but to embrace the God of love who is hidden within it.

Given all of the above arguments, the reincarnationists must concede that their theory is no more scientific, logical, or humane than the Christian one-life view. We must have just as much "blind faith" to believe that we live many lives and then eventually become perfect masters as we must have to believe that we live only one life and then dwell eternally in heaven or hell. The difference between the two beliefs ultimately lies in their different sources of authority: The Christian's faith in heaven and hell is grounded in the words of Jesus Christ and the Holy Bible, whereas the reincarnationist's faith in many lives is grounded in the subjective experiences and words of men, whether he refers to them as sages, gurus, or ascended masters. As always New-Age truth is subjective and consequently relativistic. And therefore the theory of reincarnation merely panders to the already well-fed and feted self, intensifying a person's self-absorption and self-centeredness while surrounding his newfound, more subtle egotism with a sanctimonious glow.

Finally, even if reincarnation were true—and of course it's not—it's at the very least redundant, for Christ, through his death and resurrection, came to set us free. He came, he tells us, to give us eternal life if we will believe in him only: "I give [my followers] eternal life, and they shall never perish" (John 10:28). In fact, he declares, "He who believes in me will live, even though he dies; and whoever lives and believes in me will never die" (John 11:25-26). That being the case, a follower of Christ enters eternal life, eternal heaven, because of his faith in Christ. And Christ grants such freedom freely. Is there any New-Age "liberation" that can equal the liberty that Christ promises? A belief in reincarnation is therefore unnecessary, for if through Christ death is no more, then rebirth is also no more, and the explanations offered by reincarnation needn't be considered at all by the soul who is seeking union with God.

Jesus Christ liberates his followers from sin, death, and any cares about so-called rebirths. When he sets us free, we are free indeed—once and for all time. Or if I were to put it another way for the staunch reincarnationist, in giving us eternal life, Christ isn't giving us something that we already have, for if we already have it, then he couldn't give it to us. Once we have that eternal life through faith in him, that is the end of the matter. There is no more death for us, no more birth, only eternal life.

7

THE HOSTILE
TAKEOVER

CONTRARY TO POPULAR BELIEF, MOST NEW-AGERS ARE far more fanatical than even the most fanatical Christians. To fulfill the "higher purposes" of the New Age, New-Agers will unabashedly distort, misrepresent, and quote out of context the utterances of Christians. In the pursuit of their transcendental agenda, they will even rewrite history. Truly, for the New-Age devotee to be faithful to his creed, he must blindly conform to a party line that is marked by anti-Christian sentiment and propaganda.

Almost all New-Age believers insist, for example, that Christianity in its infancy included "esoteric" teachings—on reincarnation and other occult "secrets"—that early church-men, rigidly attached to their orthodoxy, later suppressed. They did so, we are told, by excising all esoterica from the Bible—no small feat of censorship considering the scads of manuscripts that were scattered all over the Roman Empire. (Actually, Gnostic and apocryphal texts, I believe, are included in the New-Agers' use of the word *Bible*.) The apostles and many early church fathers, they claim, held these "esoteric" beliefs but withheld them from the spiritually unevolved masses (Ramacharaka 203-96). Later the "esoteric" side of Christian-ity was stamped out altogether at one of the councils held between A.D. 325 and 600 (occultists, who never quote the actual conclusions of the councils, tend to disagree about the dates and also get the councils mixed up). Fortunately, according to New-Age teachers, certain occult societies have managed to preserve this "esoteric" knowledge for those few who are "advanced" enough to receive it.

Even the words of Christ aren't exempt from their text-tampering. When he says, "I and my Father are one," they use his words to argue that we are *all* one with the Father. Because like Christ we are all sons of God, they claim, we too must be fully divine in our real natures; we too must be of one being and substance with the Father. Or when Christ says, "You must be born again," they argue that—to the adepts who are wise enough to recognize the truth—he is alluding to reincarnation. If Christians try to set them straight with appeals to biblical context, they turn a deaf ear towards these "spiritual babies" who have as yet not "experienced the Truth" for themselves. In short, if challenged, these New-Age teachers suddenly become subjectivists again—indeed, enemies of reasoned argument—who reveal a dogmatism and bigotry that would have shocked even a Grand Inquisitor.

Much of this dogmatism and prejudice is self-perpetuating. Each convert to New-Age theology inherits many false assumptions and much misinformation. Although it's almost impossible to discover all the sources behind these distortions, the distortions nevertheless remain ubiquitous and consistent from one New-Age school to the next. To demonstrate just how preposterous many of these "facts" and conclusions are, Christian writers should continue to challenge them, as they have been doing in a variety of recent books on the New-Age Movement. Only by means of this continuing effort to inject Christian truth into the culture can we weaken the credibility of the New-Age gurus. In time the truth will win out.

In this chapter, however, I intend to approach the deceit

and hostility of the New-Age teachers from a different angle. I won't even try to challenge the biblical and historical falsehoods. I'm not a qualified biblical scholar or early church historian. Moreover, this book isn't about the New-Age Movement per se but about New-Age theology. I will explore, instead, the effects that such New-Age theology is having—and must continue to have—on Christianity and society as a whole. Once these effects are revealed, it will be evident, if it hasn't become evident by now, that the "esoteric" New-Age teachings are so at odds with exoteric Christianity that any widespread acceptance of the New-Age teachings must inevitably lead to the breakdown and annihilation of traditional, biblical Christianity. It should further be evident that New-Age teachers will settle for nothing less than the complete takeover of all territories of the spirit now held by Christianity. They want to number among their legions not only those who are now Christians but also all those who might otherwise, in the absence of their New-Age propaganda, become Christians.

THE EFFECTS OF NEW-AGE THEOLOGY

In this section I will outline the process by which New-Age teachings infect and destroy the Body of Christ cell by cell, sinew by sinew, limb by limb. Using five fundamental New-Age assumptions as a springboard, I will use the facts of the present to infer the circumstances of our future. I will try to predict what the dire consequences might be if these deadly viruses continue to invade our culture, both in secular and Christian circles. At times the effects will seem to overlap, but this melding of effects will only serve to make clear just how united the New-Age effort is and how disastrous the overall effect on Christianity would be if the heralds of the New-Age have their way.

False Assumption #1: "God, Who Is Everywhere, Is Already Within Each of Us; Indeed, Each of Us Is God—the One, the Absolute—in Our Real Natures"

Those who hold this view assert that our sense of separateness from God is due to ignorance, not sin. Our vain little "self" is an illusion that can be removed by the light of knowledge—knowledge of our True Self. In truth, we are already the "One without a second." *"Aham Brahmasmi"* or "I am God," we may all declare. To remove the veil of ignorance, New-Age teachers tell us, we must exert ourselves, practicing meditation and other spiritual disciplines. Little by little we will dispel the ignorance and burn up the bad karma that we ourselves have built up through many lives. Then we shall discover that we all have been, from the start, the Divinity of all our strivings.

If such a view were widely held, original sin would be denied. Most people, including many who may have at one time considered themselves Christians, would no longer believe that they were born bearing the sin of their first father, Adam, their nature itself corrupt. Instead, they would believe they had been born with their self-created karma, good and bad, superimposed upon their pure spiritual natures. In other words, although they would accept that their physical, mental, and egoic "vehicles" are defective, as yoga-Vedantins and New-Agers do now, they would believe that their Spirit, or True Self, is pure and perfect. To such believers, the process of spiritual advancement is simple: they only have to peel away the layers of ignorance, so to speak, until they find themselves to be what they have always truly been: the True Self—God, the radiant One who is pure existence, consciousness, and bliss. In other words, they can never regard themselves as sinful, just ignorant.

But clearly if original sin were denied, so then would be Christ's substitutionary atonement and salvation by grace through faith. Operating on the above assumption, people of the

New Age would no longer be able to understand how one man could have died for the sins of the whole race. Each person, according to the New-Age view, must work through his own karma; no one can do it for him. Besides, a spiritual seeker needs knowledge of his True Self, not forgiveness for the "sins" of his illusory self. Similarly, such New-Age believers wouldn't be able to comprehend the notion of salvation by grace through faith. "Salvation from what?" they would ask. God is already eternally within each person as his True Self; so it follows also that an eternal hell, from which a person might need to be saved, can't exist.

Moreover, one might merit something *like* grace, but he can't be saved, through a single act of faith, from sin and death. In fact, sin doesn't exist, according to the New-Ager, except in the form of evil karma, and death is an illusion that necessarily must repeat, life after life, until we realize our identity with God. In other words, no "God-man"—master or avatar or incarnation—has the power to bring a person to salvation in one lifetime, quite apart from the individual's spiritual worthiness and progress. "When the student is *ready*," the occultists and yoga-Vedantins insist, then and only then does "the teacher appear."

As a result, the resurrection would then be meaningless, except as the heroic act of a great and powerful "yogi." To the occultist, God didn't raise Christ from the dead; Christ, the great yogi, raised himself. And so can we at the time of our own deaths, if we raise ourselves to a high enough level of consciousness. After all, New-Agers ask, didn't Jesus say, "And greater things than these shall you do"? Christ's attainment after his death, therefore, reveals to us the possibilities of our own spiritual self-regeneration and self-mastery. In the New Age, resurrection would merely be a metaphor for our innate ability to one day transcend our own psycho-physical bondage and master nature.

But according to orthodox Christianity, God raised Christ from the dead as a sign and promise that he would one day raise all believers from the dead. Through Christ Jesus we are lifted up, and we conquer death. "And if Christ has not been raised," asserts Paul, "your faith is futile; you are still in your sins" (1 Cor. 15:17). Notice the passive verb—"has not been raised." God raised Christ; Christ, the man, didn't resurrect himself by means of a great yogic feat. Then Paul goes on to explain the significance of the resurrection and its final outcome:

> But Christ has indeed been raised from the dead, the first-fruits of those who have fallen asleep. For since death came through a man, the resurrection of the dead comes also through a man. For as in Adam all die, so in Christ all will be made alive. But each in his own turn: Christ, the first-fruits; then, when he comes, those who belong to him. Then the end will come, when he hands over the kingdom to God the Father after he has destroyed all dominion, authority and power.
> —1 Cor. 15:20-24

Of course, the New-Age believer, whether sympathetic to Christ or not, would have to deny these words, regarding them as mere "theologizing" and not at all based on "spiritual experience." How could he conceive of such total submission to Christ, in whom "all *will be made* alive," and such absolute faith in a second coming when Christ will return to separate the tares from the wheat, the sheep from the goats, raising his devotees to life and sending the unbelievers, wailing and gnashing their teeth, to eternal punishment?

Furthermore, if each of us is God and doesn't need a "savior" outside of ourselves, then Christ's call to spread his Gospel (Matt. 28:19-20) becomes meaningless. Missionary zeal would cease to exist if Christ were to become nothing more than one great master whose cross symbolizes self-sacrifice and transcendence rather than substitutionary atonement and salvation by grace through faith. Similarly, the joy of salvation would be diminished, if not destroyed, if the resurrection were stripped of its mighty power to remake and renew the whole man, making him dead to the world and the world dead to him. According to New-Agers, Christ doesn't save, justify, sanctify, and glorify us; he merely shows us how we can save, justify, sanctify, and glorify ourselves. He merely points the way and guides us in our efforts to be free of the apparently endless cycles of birth and death. In this way, he is *a way* but not the *only way*.

Finally, if New-Age believers were to live as though everything is in substance already God—having come out of him as a web comes out of a spider—then everything would be regarded as sacred, and evil would cease to be evil. Distinctions would be confused and blurred. An owl, a fish, or a tree, for example, would have the same rights as a man, woman, or child. The corps of engineers wouldn't be permitted to build a dam that would save the property and lives of thousands of humans, lest they drive a score of hawks from their nests along a river. In time, devotees themselves, declaring that "Everything is an illusion, and God alone exists," would hardly notice the mass murder of millions of unborn babies except as so many strange wrinkles in the silken fabric of God. But while strolling along the sidewalk, the enlightened New-Ager would hesitate to step on a caterpillar lest he snuff out a sacred life. In time, relativism would reign supreme throughout Christendom—or at least what used to be called Christendom. And hocus pocus, everything would be out of focus, except to the "knower of God" who would sit idly all day while the world plunged toward destruction, radiating the "Truth" that all is God, all is one. A perverse kind of peace would rule in the hearts of men.

And at the peaceful center of all these consequences, we may find Satan smirking, exulting over his greatest victory to date: the obliteration of man's sense of sin. Aided by New-Age theology, he has effectively stripped sin of its sinfulness and thus has driven a wedge between modern man and the Gospel of Christ. In this way, the path has been cleared for the next New-Age "truth."

*False Assumption #2: "Truth Is Relative Because
Everything Other Than God, the Absolute, Is Relative
(That Is, Impermanent and Changeable)"*

If accepted as true, this assumption would deny three types of traditional authority. First, people who base their beliefs on this assumption would have to view the Bible as a historical document consisting of many relatively true pronouncements and values—inspiring, of course, but unreliable as a source of truth in the modern world. In time these advanced New-Age thinkers, many of them perhaps Christians, would have to conclude that the Bible as an objective, infallible authority—even in matters of faith and morals—is of little value at all.

Second, they would have to deny the authority of the Church, for if the Bible is flawed and flawed theologians over the centuries have based their theology on the questionable authority of the Bible, the very teachings of the Church must be only relatively true. As a consequence, people would no longer feel any allegiance to the Church or even to local churches, except perhaps as social clubs. And who would need a social club that survives by begging for the hard-earned money of its members when he can find the truth within himself, his own truth?

Third, and worst of all, many people, thus bitten by the bug of relativism, would begin to question the authority and uniqueness of Christ himself. The fact that Christ lived two thousand years ago would weigh heavily against him, for as a man of his age, he would have been, according to modern thinking, limited by the values and knowledge of his age. Besides, as the enlightened would argue, because the Bible was written two thousand years ago by ignorant men, we can't be sure that the recorded words of Christ are really his words at all.

As a result, subjectivism and its evil twin, relativism, would be further exalted in our age. A believer would have to decide for himself, based on his own spiritual intuitions (derived from the

"Christ-Consciousness" within him), which truths would and wouldn't apply to him or his circumstances. He would be constantly on the lookout for "universal" spiritual laws that extend or transcend the teachings of the Bible, a book that he would now have to interpret symbolically. Hell, for example, would have to be a state of mind, not a place; it would be a metaphor for a temporary state encountered on the way to union with the Absolute. As for the applications of spiritual laws for other people, the New-Age believer would have to leave others alone to work out their own salvation, to do their own thing as long as they didn't hurt anybody. "If it feels right," the New-Age minister would have to say, "do it. Just follow your heart, and listen to the Christ within."

But if all truths were viewed as relative, we wouldn't really have any moral or spiritual laws to guide our steps. There can't be law where lawlessness reigns, where each is a law unto himself. In time relativism would result in nihilism and social chaos. The vast majority of people, content to leave the philosophizing and theologizing to others, would simply lapse into a spiritual and moral coma, incapable of distinguishing between right and wrong. As for orthodox Christians, they would have to huddle around truths that would be only "relatively true." In doing so, they would be, like passengers on a spiritual *Titanic*, clinging to a sinking ship in a turbulent sea.

Although sad, many mainline churches today are already foundering in this way. Only a few years ago when I was contemplating entering a seminary on the West Coast, I asked a minister there about his church's stand on homosexuality, since I had heard from seminarians themselves that a few homosexuals were living with their "significant others" in the dorms of the seminary. He replied quite offhandedly and tolerantly that he had no problem with the practice and then, sensing my disapproval, authoritatively added, "Of course, we now know that Paul's catalog of sins in Romans 1 is outdated. Homosexuality is a valid lifestyle. Homosexuals don't choose their orientation; they are born that way."

Given the current research into genetics, one can just as easily argue that alcoholics and certain kinds of pathological criminals don't choose their behaviors either. Does that make their behavior moral? Are they then absolved of moral responsibility for their conduct? Of course not. We insist that they receive treatment or pay for their misbehavior. But morality has very little to do with those arguments that condone homosexuality, that declare that this or any other perversion of God's law is a valid lifestyle. For now, ministers like the one I interviewed still call themselves Christians—that is, "followers of Christ." But for how much longer will they be able to do so without altering the traditional definition of "Christian" and broadening the way of the cross into a four-lane superhighway?

Unfortunately, that new path, comprised of many paths, has already been blazed. Thousands are treading it even as you read, accepting without question the next New-Age "truth."

False Assumption #3: "All Paths Lead to the Same God"

"Oh, yes, Christ is one of the avatars." Swami S. used to tell me this is how Hindus respond to Christian missionaries. On the walls of their family shrines Hindus display pictures of Jesus, on the cross or in the arms of Mary, side by side with pictures of the Buddha, Guru Nanak, Kali, and Hanuman. New-Age teachers, in the same way, would have us level Jesus, strip him of his exclusive claim to Sonship. He would then merely become "the Christ-Consciousness," something within each of us, to which each of us has ready access if we exert ourselves properly and attune ourselves to the teaching of the ascended masters—or even the goddess who resides within nature as Mother of us all. When Christ is understood in this "universal" light, the seeker no longer needs external props or authorities—ministers or pastors, the Church, the Bible, or even the historical Jesus Christ. He simply needs to submit to a New-Age guru, a set of instructions, or—better yet— his "inner guide" and perceive the one in the many—God manifesting himself in all the religions of the world, in all people in search of God, and of course in the person himself, where Christ already dwells with his nonjudgmental, unconditional love, accepting all "wherever they're coming from." All we really need, then, is love; all we really need is love.

With such a belief in the truth and oneness of all paths, even apparently worldly paths, why would anyone promote one path over another? Why would Christians preach the Gospel at all in India and China, where Hinduism and Buddhism reign? Why would Christians exhort New-Agers, pop psychologists, or even the witches of WICCA to follow Christ as their Lord and Savior? What would be the point in quoting Jesus—"I am the way and the truth and the life. No one comes to the Father except through me" (John 14:6)? If missionaries did indeed go forth in the name of the New Universal Religion of the New Age, they would be preaching a new gospel, not the Gospel of Jesus Christ. Hence, in such a world Christianity as the Way of Christ would no longer exist as it has existed for nearly two thousand years.

Only a vitiated, anemic Christianity would remain, a path for old fogies afraid of the new freedom afforded them by New-Age theology. According to the wisdom of the New Age, conservative Christians would prove the truth of Emerson's dictum: "A foolish consistency is the hobgoblin of little minds." Because they wouldn't be able to live with the new world vision of unity in diversity—"As many faiths, so many paths," they would be regarded as hopelessly unenlightened. Incapable of yielding an inch, the remaining died-in-the-wool Christians would never be able to see the New-Age religion as anything more than an eclectic smorgasbord of contradictions. Many of us who now still cling to Christ and his Church would be numbered among these feeble-minded folk—tolerated but ridiculed for their parochialism and chauvinism. The enlightened would shake their heads, even as they do now, at us "spiritual babies" who still insist on living in the old age, the Piscean Age, attached to our dogmas, props, and childish prayers. For our own good and the good of the world, they would have to erase any trace of the anachronistic Christian God from government, the schools, and the family.

As two prophets of the New Age, TV news reporters on a local station, recently put it when referring to Christmas, "This time of year means many things to many people, and so we wish everyone happiness during this holiday season." They only needed to add after the word "happiness" the phrase "in their own way" to make the New-Age appeal complete.

With these first three false assumptions firmly established, people will then, if New-Agers have their way, be prepared to understand and apply two even higher "truths."

False Assumption #4: "All Persons Will Achieve
Self-realization (or God-consciousness) After Many
Births Through Self-effort and the Assistance
of the Unerring Law of Karma"

By now, the pattern of effects should be clear: orthodox Christianity would be gutted, neutralized, rendered inoffensive by New-Age theology. In the course of its rise to ascendancy, New-Age theology would obliterate the idea of sin and deny our need for a personal God and for his grace. We would become self-sufficient subjectivists, as many in America already are. On our own terms, but cognizant of the law of karma, we would create our own futures and at the same time remain true to our goal, as long as we kept our sights set on the attainment of the God within, who is also without, who is indeed everywhere as our greatest ally in our struggle to realize him. Having no need of Christianity, we would be free to experiment with diverse approaches within the workshops of our own souls. If everything is God, everything is holy, and everything leads to God, then we would be free to find him wherever we wish. In the long course of evolution there might be, to be sure, some setbacks. But there can be no failures because everyone must eventually arrive at the same point—God, regardless of where each person starts or how he proceeds.

Thus, the spread of New-Age theology would fuel the proliferation of new "methods of attainment." For a while some would practice yoga, then perhaps TM, Zen, Eckankar, or meditation on crystals. Because all religions would be regarded as true, methods used the world over would have to be sampled, "integrated holistically" into the spiritual life of each seeker as he sees fit. People would become more and more preoccupied with their own subjective states as they adjust and fine-tune their psyches—Rolfing their bodies, getting in touch with their inner child, opening themselves to higher influences. Who then would need a personal God, the God of Abraham, Isaac, and Jacob, of David, Isaiah, and Jesus Christ?

The final result would be the exaltation of the age-old original sin: pride. Because spiritual seekers will know that they can become God, equal to God in life, light, and love, they will be proud of their equanimity and serenity, of their self-control and purity, of their wisdom and "level of attainment." No doubt, they will even be proud of their humility. In time, we would be surrounded by plaster saints and gurus on every corner. We would have a universal, generic macho spirituality based on a broad-minded smarmy toleration of all people—except, of course, orthodox Christians (especially when they preach that Jesus Christ is the only way, a truth that Christ himself preached).

What, then, is left to understand? Once the earnest New-Age seekers have understood the first three foundational "truths" and then the penultimate "truth," they have only to grasp and apply the ultimate New-Age "truth."

False Assumption #5: "The Supreme Goal of Life is Self-realization"

Already in our society, people declare that the highest goal of life is self-fulfillment and that nothing else matters. To enter the New Age, we must simply build on the already-established groundwork of secular humanism. To do so, we have only to spiritualize the term "self-fulfillment," removing the taint of selfishness from it, and substitute for it "Self-realization," and we will have ennobled a decades-old "truth" advocated by pop psychologists. Still, even with this spiritualizing, the assumption is hardly harmless. It remains just as narcissistic in its emphasis and as pernicious in its effects as any pronouncement made by pop psychologists.

First and foremost, the widespread acceptance and application of this final assumption would destroy traditional human bonds, beginning with the family. Why? Because living with others—meeting one's obligations, fulfilling one's duties to them—would be regarded as a distraction from the real business of living. How, after all, could one raise his consciousness and establish himself in an unshakable equanimity if he were constantly interrupted by the demands of children and spouse or aging parents? Besides, these other people have to work out their own karma and find their own paths to God, right? Spiritual development or liberation would become a person's private, most central concern, and "detachment" his watchword. As a result, he would be concerned almost exclusively with how he feels at any given moment in relation to his struggle for Self-realization.

In time, then, this self-centered loner would also ignore or cease to make commitments—marital and filial ones, for instance—for the sake of his own "spiritual progress" or "psychic development." In doing so, he would forget two fundamental Christian truths that enable us to see our duties as binding and sacred:

*"[W]hoever wants to become great among you must be your
servant, and whoever wants to be first must be your slave—
just as the Son of Man did not come to be served, but to
serve, and to give his life as a ransom for many."*
—Matt. 20:26-28

*"My command is this: Love each other as I have loved you.
Greater love has no one than this, that one lay down his life
for his friends."*
—John 15:12-13

But such self-sacrifice for the sake of others, even one's family
members, would seem impractical to a New-Age seeker. Why
should he serve others unless it's going to enhance his own spiritual advancement? He is a light-bearer, a benefactor to humanity. Others should listen to him and give him due respect. They
should fall at his feet and feel themselves fortunate. He is much
too busy to deal with details—runny noses, meal preparation,
empathy. Let the world cater to his needs and accept him as he
is—or be gone from his sight. Spouse, parents, brothers, and sisters—he will bless them in their quest for Self-realization, as he
must; but he will tell them to fend for themselves and will remain
blissfully impassive in the face of their tribulations.

In time, after the traditional sense of family thus breaks
down, the sense of duty toward those outside the family would
also break down. Why would the New-Age seeker feel bound by
social obligations any more than he felt bound by familial obligations? Why would he attend church and serve others when he
can find God within himself and radiate God's peace to the world
no matter where he is? Why would he empathize with others
when empathizing would wreak havoc with his "holy" mood
and threaten his centeredness, throwing him off-balance, perhaps
even damaging his self-esteem? Because New-Age seekers believe
that people create their own karma and must work through that

karma from their own levels of consciousness, they simply have to ignore a certain amount of suffering in the world, just as they have ignored the needs and wants of their families. For the sake of their own spiritual development, they might engage in some charitable works, but they would always remember that they shouldn't interfere in the karma of others. After all, anyone who is suffering has brought his own suffering upon himself because of his ignorance of his True Self—the God Within.

In short, in the new New-Age world without missionaries and charitable organizations founded on Christian principles, the advanced souls would largely "do their own thing," unconstrained by guilt or a self-sacrificing compassion. Acts of charity would then have to be left to the machinery of the welfare state, but that would be fine with the New-Age seeker. He would rather not soil his hands with the details or distract his mind from his goal. No matter what the cost, he would have to remain wholly committed to his grand multi-life project: his own illumination. As for the rest of the world, it had better move out of his way. There are already far too many slowpokes on the highway of life to suit him.

Then society, undermined by all the above assumptions, would begin to crumble. Divorce rates would continue to skyrocket, to be sure, but a new phenomenon would also appear. More and more people would never marry because they would see no spiritual advantage in it. They would leap into and out of relationships to find their "soul mates" or to burn up their karma with one insignificant other after another, all in the name of their single-minded effort to liberate themselves from the clutches of maya. And such relationships might be heterosexual or homosexual since people would "know" that they have lived many lives, as men *and* women, and thus have many complex relational lessons to learn. Without a doubt, crime rates would also increase as most people, freed from the constraints of biblical Christianity, discover that they can do as they please, as long as they think they are working out their karma and seeking wholeness. And finally, as individual initiative diminishes—as surely it must in the new *otherworldly* world—poverty and injustice would spread throughout the land and become the norm, as it already has in India, the birthplace of New-Age theology. History would no longer be regarded as progressive, leading to the establishment of God's kingdom on earth, but cyclical, leading nowhere.

Thus, in this onrushing New Age, the old self would remain just as stubborn and resistant to God as it always has been, except that now it would wear a capital "S" to dignify and conceal its corruption. In this way the stage would be set for the appearance of the most serenely detached, most supremely Self-realized master of all masters, the one who will possess enough occultic power to unite all peoples and save the world from destruction: the antichrist, whose coming was predicted two thousand years ago by the apostles John (1 John 2:18; Rev. 13) and Paul (2 Thess. 2).

NEW-AGE RESPONSES

How might sensitive New-Age theologians attempt to dismiss these unflattering charges and dire predictions? From my experiences with yoga-Vedanta and Western Occultism, I would say they would offer three responses.

"Christians, We Have Come in Peace"

First, they would say that the truths they preach are only intended for the advanced few, not the unprepared, unevolved masses. "We don't mean to destroy Christianity or anyone's faith," they would say, brows knitted earnestly, hands folded in their laps. "We only want to reach those who are at or near our level of consciousness."

Clearly, however, considering the proliferation of New-Age books, teachers, classes, psychic fairs, and conferences in recent

166 \ EMBRACED BY THE DARKNESS

years, New-Agers are aggressively seeking converts. With their teachings, they have invaded bookstores, board rooms, and even school rooms (Groothuis, *Confronting*). So no matter what they say to the contrary, they obviously want to disseminate their truths to the many, because they think these "higher truths" are good for people and society. If they didn't intend to reform Christianity or replace it with their own views, they would be content to keep their truths confined to their secret societies, allowing themselves to mysteriously appear as teachers when the students were ready. Why won't they admit to what everyone else knows to be human nature? Anyone who possesses what he believes to be the truth will always feel inclined to convince others of its value. Otherwise, of what use is his truth? New-Agers do indeed want to convert the world to their way of thinking. Unfortunately, Christianity stands in their way, and for that reason they despise it.

"We Have Come Not to Destroy but to Revise Christianity"

Second, Christianity, they might argue, has been wrong from the start, having distorted or hidden the true teachings of Christ. Therefore, it has been built on misinterpretations and humbug. Christians, in other words, don't really worship the true Christ, Christ as he really is; and so a major revision of Christianity would be good for everyone.

But to maintain this position, New-Age theologians would have to be hypocrites because they tell us again and again that all paths are true—all lead to God. If that is the case, then orthodox Christianity must be true also. Christians who earnestly follow Jesus Christ, loving God with all their hearts, minds, souls, and strength and loving their neighbors as themselves, are also, by New-Age definition, on the high road to God. For this reason, New-Agers shouldn't condemn or disturb the faith, doctrines, or dogmas of Christians. They should respect Christians and count them as brothers and sisters in God, even when Christians oppose them. Therefore, when New-Agers tamper with the essential beliefs of Christianity or try to revise them along New-Age lines, they are not only acting inconsistently with their beliefs but are waging a war against Christianity. Nothing less than the destruction of Christianity could be their motive and purpose.

"We Only Mean to Show You the True Teachings of Christ"

Finally, and probably most likely, New-Age theologians would argue that Christ himself approves of the New-Age truths because they are his truths. Why else would they keep invoking the terms "Christ Self" and "Christ-Consciousness"? Why else would they keep quoting Scripture in support of their position? Some Christians might contend that New-Age theologians are simply thieves and liars who use the name and words of Christ to deceive the unwary. But let's assume for the moment that the New-Age teachers are sincere and guileless. Obviously, in that case they must believe they are advocating the will of Christ. Therefore, they must also believe that Christ approves of their dismantling of orthodox Christianity, a dismantling that would have the far-reaching and terrifying effects already discussed above. The destruction of orthodox Christianity shouldn't seem an inappropriate goal to them; after all, its founding, according to their analysis of history, was fundamentally flawed.

However, whatever their position, Jesus Christ most certainly couldn't favor the dismantling of orthodox Christianity. Why would he have presented specific teachings, elaborated upon by his disciples, and preserved the Church and the Scriptures during persecutions and other threats for two thousand years, only to reverse himself at this bewildering point in history? Would he really say, in effect, "I'm sorry, but I didn't mean what I said when I spoke urgently and passionately about eternal hell-fire and Judgment Day and referred to myself as the only way"? Or,

"You've had it wrong from the beginning—I'm so sorry that I didn't help you get it right." Or, "Here—these are my new and improved teachings, so forget all that other stuff—except, of course, the parts about love."

If such were the case, millions of believers would have their faith destroyed and their moral compasses demagnetized, not all at once, of course, but over time—just as it's happening now in Europe and America. In this sense, New-Age theologians, though perhaps unwittingly, are as much the enemies of Christ as are secular humanists and atheists. In effect, they are declaring that over the centuries all the martyrs have died for the wrong reasons and the great theologians have drawn the wrong conclusions.

But if Christ doesn't approve of the destruction of Christianity, then obviously his will doesn't really matter to New-Age theologians. They are merely using the name of Christ—and not at all relying on the real Person, Jesus Christ— to lend legitimacy to their views. In point of fact, it's their own agenda, not the will of Christ, that matters to them. After all, according to their own admission Jesus Christ is just one of many great Sons of God. Perhaps his time of influence has passed: the one universal Ancient Wisdom lives forever, but the Sons of God come and go. In the final analysis, New-Age teachers must tell us the truth. They actually believe that we are evolving beyond Christianity and no longer have need of the historical Christ.

THE FORCE BEHIND THE NEW-AGE CONVICTIONS

So what do the New-Age teachings about Jesus Christ and Christianity reduce themselves to? Lies. And like the father of lies, lies destroy; they are rooted in diabolism, not divinity. In short, the force behind New-Age theology, being wantonly destructive, must be evil.

"Evil," according to the psychiatrist M. Scott Peck, ". . . is that force, residing either inside or outside human beings, that seeks to kill life or liveliness" (*People of the Lie* 43). Contrast this definition with the mission of Christ: "I have come to fulfill not to destroy" and "I have come to give life and give it more abundantly." New-Age theology, by its very nature, must kill the life and liveliness of Christianity and Christians, for if the New-Age global plan of "unity in diversity" were to become a reality, the result would be the destruction of Christianity. So let no one claim that the teachings of the New Age complement those of Christ when actually they radically contradict them. From Madame Blavatsky to Elizabeth Clare Prophet, New-Age prophets have always had one bias in common: they detest orthodox Christianity, the Christianity that is grounded in Scripture and tradition.

Having been at one time a New-Age seeker myself, I am aware that some of my New-Age readers will be bemused by my suggestion that the force behind their beliefs is demonic. Others, however, will most certainly be outraged. To the former, I can say nothing; their convictions are unshakable. To the latter, however, I can say that their anger actually reflects their ambivalence toward the words of Christ and the doctrines of the Church. For such people, a spark of hope exists. Their anger and defensiveness reflect not the way children of God react to the beneficent and perfect Savior, but the way demons, sensing a threat to their oppressive rule, react to him. All around such people, a veritable host of demons rages against the Father, Son, and Holy Spirit to conceal from them the fact that they are still capable of responding to the words of Christ. For such I pray, as Christians once prayed for me when I was plunged into a darkness that I believed to be light. In the meantime, let no one forget that Satan is also an angel of light, having been the chief of all the angels and a great light himself—hence, his name Lucifer ("son of the morning"). Darkness, therefore, can and does masquerade as light.

Finally, if some readers find this talk about Satan and his demons unacceptable because it seems too simplistic, then they have landed themselves on a slippery slope, for if they confront the historical Jesus in the New Testament, they would have to conclude that he himself was a simpleton because he, too, believed that Satan and his host of demons exist and strive for the minds, hearts, and souls of men. If such New-Age devotees can't accept the words of Jesus as they relate to the reality of Satan, they also can't truly and fully accept his words as they relate to himself—to his own divinity and world mission. They would be incapable of accepting on faith the reality of Jesus Christ *qua* Jesus Christ, the *only* Son of God, who died for all of us upon the cross to save us from sin and death and to give us eternal life. If such is the case, from now on let all New-Age devotees no longer use the name of Jesus Christ if they are unwilling to believe in him or accept his words. If they can't accept his absolute authority over their lives—their bodies, minds, souls, and, yes, even *wills*—then let them banish him from their theology and spiritual lives altogether and forever.

So let the battle lines be clearly drawn—and without delay, for the dire effects of which I have spoken in this chapter are already upon us, sweeping over us like locusts blackening the sky and blotting out the sun. In light of the evidence before us, it takes no prophet to predict our future.

8

A LAST METAPHYSICAL GASP

WHAT DO ANIMISM AND ASTROLOGY HAVE IN COMmon? They are both superstitions. Even though few today would mount a case for animism, many would argue vehemently that astrology is a science, a source of truth and wisdom dating back to the ancient Hindus, Egyptians, Persians, and Greeks and promoted by such luminaries as Thoth, Pythagoras, Hippocrates, Ptolemy, Kepler, Copernicus, and more recently Michel Gauguelin, a French psychologist and statistician, and Dr. Percy Seymour, a lecturer in astronomy at the Plymouth Polytechnic Institute in England. So certain is the faith of New-Agers in astrology that they accord it a major place in their theology: it's not only a predictive tool but a path to wisdom. Indeed, the whole New-Age Movement is based upon a belief in astrology because it was from astrology that the term "New Age" arose. The irony, of course, is that if astrology is false, then the "New Age" never was, nor will it ever be, at least not as New-Agers conceive of it.

The ancient tradition of astrology isn't so ancient, though; nor is the present evidence in favor of astrology so impressive. Even though astrologers claim that the roots of astrology are ancient, Jim Tester in his book *A History of Western Astrology* demonstrates that astrology has more modern origins. It was the

Hellenistic Greeks who actually perfected the mathematical portion of astrology: "The twelve [signs] from Aries to Pisces seemed to have emerged as standard from no earlier than the end of the fifth century B.C., and the first mention of twelve equal signs, as opposed to the constellations (of unequal extent in the heavens), was 419 B.C." (14). He claims there is no evidence, as New-Agers would have us believe, of a more ancient Egyptian astrology, except in a *very* crude form. Even the earliest of "the few known Babylonian horoscopes is dated 410 B.C., and the great mass of horoscopes preserved from ancient times, all Greek, belong to the first five centuries of our era" (12).

Over the centuries of astrology's development from Hellenistic times to the present, astrologers have also vigorously disagreed about many basic matters: house divisions, the relative importance of conception and birth, the influence of the fixed stars, and the significance of the fixed and moving zodiacs (211). Although a few scientists such as Kepler tinkered with astrology, most, such as Bacon, thought it full of superstition or, such as Newton, showed little interest in it (218-35).

Today the situation hasn't changed much. Scientists still debunk astrology because they know that it's unscientific and riddled with inexplicable inconsistencies. Already the scientific community has dismissed as seriously flawed the recent work of Michel Gauguelin, who tried to show that there is a statistical correlation between planetary positions at birth and one's choice of vocation. And the work of Dr. Percy Seymour, although interesting, as yet offers no proof that astrology is valid. He has only proven that the electromagnetic field around the earth fluctuates as solar activity occurs and that certain creatures on the earth are sensitive to these fluctuations.

Yet despite its shaky origins and questionable status as a science, astrology is at the heart of the New-Age Movement in the Western world, for the concept of the New Age is based entirely on the notion that we are entering the Age of Aquarius. Based on a belief in this concept, fatuous songs have been written ("This is the dawning of the Age of Aquarius") and people have flocked to gurus and "harmonic convergences." Based on a belief in this concept, too, New-Age teachers have told us that because of the influence of Uranus, the so-called ruler of Aquarius, we are about to enter a new era of unprecedented wisdom, brotherhood, and true spirituality, unfettered by the dogmas of the Piscean Age, the age during which Christianity reigned supreme. Now Christianity, they tell us, is passé. With the dawning of the New Age, all true believers will follow a nondogmatic, universal spiritual path.

And today, true to the influence of Aquarius—and the electric, eclectic vibrations of Uranus—New-Age teachers and proselytes are giddy with anticipation, quite willing to hearken to their ancient sources of wisdom while rejecting out of hand the prophets of the Old Testament and the salvation offered by the Christ of the New Testament. They can't accept the biblical position—namely, that astrology and other forms of divination are evil. They can't even accept, at the very least, that these "arts" usurp, as Augustine argued, the authority that the will of God should assume in a person's life. Those who would be masters of themselves, those who seek to be God, believe they have every right to perceive and alter the future. Why, when they can read the heavens and rule their own destinies, should they rely on the providential care and mercy of a Father in heaven?

THE GROUNDLESSNESS OF ASTROLOGY

Actually, however, traditional astrology has no basis in scientific fact, nor is it even rational. Three of the most cherished underpinnings of astrology, in fact, can easily be proven false: the existence of the zodiac, the influences of the planets, and the symbolic validity of astrology.

The Existence of the Zodiac

The zodiac is an imaginary belt, divided into twelve equal signs of thirty degrees each, that supposedly surrounds the earth. (Actually, as Figure 1 shows, the earth's somewhat elliptical path around the sun forms the zodiac.) Of the twelve signs, four are said to be cardinal: Aries, Cancer, Libra, and Capricorn. Aries, the first sign, launches the cycle of the zodiac, its zero degree appearing on about March 21, the vernal equinox. The influence of Aries lasts for about thirty days, a period that coincides roughly with the thirty degrees of the sign. Cancer, the fourth sign, appears on the summer solstice; Libra, the seventh sign, on the autumnal equinox; and Capricorn, the tenth sign, on the winter solstice. As a result, each of these cardinal signs, along with the two that follow it, acquires some of the qualities of its corresponding season.

Aries, the first sign of spring, for example, is supposed to be the sign of initiatory action and aggressiveness; Taurus, the next spring sign, of sensuousness and robust vitality; and so on. Because each sign may be regarded as a kind of energy field, everything on the earth during the rule of a sign, especially each person, bears the unmistakable stamp of that season-bound sign. All the signs together, so runs the theory, are supposed to represent a cyclical pattern of "energies" that the sensitive astrologer grasps intuitively (Rudhyar 38-39; George 25ff.).

However, encircling our zodiac and solar system are the far, far distant constellations, from which the signs of the zodiac have received their names and their attributes. Sagittarius, represented by the Archer, for example, inclines those who are born under it toward idealism, philosophy, higher education, and the attainment of great goals. Like archers, they shoot for the hawk overhead or the distant boar in the bush. Unfortunately, when it comes to the actual correspondence between the constellational and zodiacal signs, modern astrologers have a problem: the zero

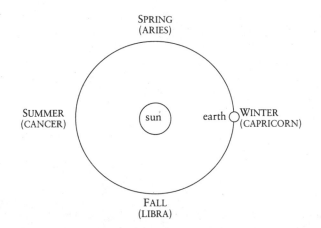

Figure 1. Imaginary Belt Formed by the Earth's Path Around the Sun
and the Four Cardinal Points

degree of the constellational Aries doesn't align with the zero
degree of the zodiacal Aries. As Figure 2 illustrates, the zero
degree of the one is in fact now separated from the zero degree
of the other by about twenty-two degrees, so that the vernal
equinox on earth (Aries) actually corresponds with about the
eighth degree of the constellation Pisces. In several years, as the
point of the vernal equinox seems to move backwards against the
constellations, it will correspond with seven degrees of Pisces,
then six degrees, and so on. So if a person is born on, say, April
1, is he, according to heavenly influences, an Aries (rough and
tough) or a Pisces (meek and mild)? The Hindus, who adhere to
the constellational signs but disregard the season-bound zodiacal signs, say Pisces; Western astrologers, who quite sensibly disregard the influences of the too-distant constellations, say Aries.

What causes this apparent discrepancy between the constellations and zodiacal signs with the same names? Why don't the
sidereal (stellar) and zodiacal degrees coincide? At fault is a scientifically observable phenomenon: the precession of the earth's
equinoxes against the star-studded sky. According to *Webster's*,
the precession of the equinoxes may be defined as "the occur-

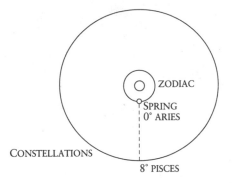

Figure 2. Earth Against the Apparent Circle of the Distant Constellations. Because the earth wobbles, 0° Aries isn't at the exact point each year along the earth's path around the sun. By comparison, the constellations appear to be fixed.

rence of the equinoxes earlier in each successive sidereal year, caused by the gradual westward movement of the equinoctial points along the ecliptic as the result of the change in direction of the earth's axis as it turns around the axis of the ecliptic so as to describe a complete cone approximately every 26,000 years." Put simply, the earth isn't a perfect circle, and its north and south poles aren't perfectly vertical in relation to its path around the sun. Earth is tilted slightly, so it wobbles, so to speak, as it revolves around the sun. (Note the position of the equator in Figure 3.)

Consequently, over time, the zero degree of the zodiacal Aries and the zero degree of the constellational (or sidereal) Aries appear to slip farther and farther apart, until they are 180 degrees apart, then closer and closer until they coincide again. This cycle of aligning, separating, and realigning requires 26,000 years to complete. At present, then, as was already mentioned, the zero degree of zodiacal Aries, which marks the beginning of spring, has slipped back to the eighth degree of the constellation Pisces—and Arians may actually be Pisceans, Pisceans Aquarians, and so on.

Now, then, given the precession of the equinoxes, we are pre-

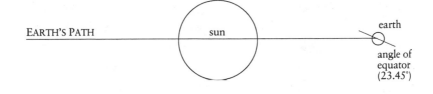

Figure 3. Plane of the Earth's Path Around the Sun. When the earth is tilted on its axis away from the sun, it's winter in the Northern Hemisphere, summer in the Southern Hemisphere.

pared to understand the origin of the term "New Age"—or "The Age of Aquarius." Because astrologers assign to the cusps or transition points of the twelve signs (the zero- or thirty-degree point of each sign) an orb of influence of eight degrees, they tell us that on a cosmic scale we—as a civilization hurtling through space on a wobbling planet—are now on the cusp of the constellation Aquarius. That is, we are part of a cosmic countdown, measured by the movement of the zero-degree of zodiacal Aries backward through the constellations. In only eight more degrees—or in well over five hundred years!—the zero degree of the zodiacal Aries will cross over an invisible mathematical line into the constellation of Aquarius. Then, a little over two thousand years later, it will slip into Capricorn and a new more serious age will be born in which everyone wears Armani suits and exclaims, "Like a goat, I'm going to hot-hoof my way to the top."

In the meantime, astrologers tell us, we are now enjoying the first influences of Aquarius. Hence we are witnessing the "dawning of the New Age." And of course the really evolved people are already cooperating with the new vibes, de-genderizing the world, declaring, "I'm okay, you're okay," and becoming politically—or, should I say, evolutionarily—correct.

This theory of ages, however, makes no sense. For one thing it isn't clear how we, singly or collectively, can feel the influences of the constellations at all when surely they must be blocked out by the much more powerful "influences" of the zodiacal signs and planets. Surely we must be as insensible to constellational radiations as a man inside an electrical plant would be to radio signals being broadcast from Mars when his only receiver is a metal plate in his head. How could our situation be otherwise, given the vastness of the universe? Moreover, the whole system is so arbitrary. Who named the constellations? Why did certain ancient graybeards see a virgin rather than a lamp, or a centaur instead of a camel? Some ancients held that there were four signs, others that there were eighteen (Tester 14). Who decided on twelve? Who decided at what point the constellational circle begins when it could have begun anywhere? It's all incomprehensible.

The whole fiction of the zodiac really disintegrates, however, when one huge scientifically verifiable inconsistency is brought to light. If the vernal equinox marks the beginning of Aries, defining and empowering it, then how are we to regard the vernal equinox of those who live in the Southern Hemisphere, say, the Australians, whose seasons—and thus equinoxes—are the opposite of ours in the Northern Hemisphere? (Again refer to Figure 3.) If that half of the world is experiencing Aries, their vernal equinox, when we are experiencing Libra, our autumnal equinox, does that mean the civilization below the equator is actually on the cusp of the Age of Leo, the sign opposite Aquarius? After all, the zero degree of their Aries is approaching Leo, not Aquarius. Confusing, isn't it? To make matters worse, such an Age of Leo wouldn't be an age of peace and brotherhood, like the Age of Aquarius, but one of fiery creativity and rivaling monarchies. So should we Americans be on our guard? Napoleon's sun lay near the end of Cancer, within seven degrees of Leo—namely, on its cusp. What might this bit of history tell us? Just as we in the Northern Hemisphere are yearning for world peace and unity, the Australians will be yearning for world domination. Before long, we shall all be roasting 'roos on the barbee and slugging down Foster's like Purelated tap water.

Thus the zodiac doesn't exist, certainly not in any scientific or logical sense, for how can a scientific or logical system—that is, one that is universally true—be applied to only half the world? The "energy" belt of the zodiac can't have two beginnings, two points called zero-degree Aries, one for us and one for them.

The Influence of the Planets

But if the fiction of the zodiac disappears, what remains? At this point astrologers might try to salvage their pseudo-science by directing our attention to the bodies within our solar system. Trotting out such terms as "electromagnetism" and "gravitational force," they will insist that the planets influence us. Let's examine this astrological theory and then consider it in light of the scientific evidence.

Astrologers claim that each planet from Mercury to Pluto, the two "luminaries" (the sun and moon), and even comets and asteroids shed their own vibrations. They are sources of energies that interrelate, sometimes harmonizing, sometimes polarizing, sometimes conflicting with each other, forming a kind of solar-systemic grid. And the earth, as well as all that lives upon it, is a recipient of all these influences. People, especially, although they still have free will, follow certain predictable patterns based on the configurations at their births and the ongoing process of planetary interactions in the solar system. The astrologers speak of these cause-and-effect relationships between planets and the affairs of men as though they can be verified scientifically.

To explain how these cause-and-effect relationships work, astrologers refer to planetary aspects. From the earth, they say, the planets appear to form relationships based on their distances from one another. If in the sky Venus, for example, is 120 degrees from Jupiter, the aspect is said to be good or favorable; if Saturn is ninety degrees from Mars, however, the aspect is said to be evil or unfavorable. The whole matter is even further complicated when astrologers tell us that certain planets are malevolent or beneficent, that planets above or below the earth's horizon incline people toward inner or outer activity, that signs color the natural dispositions of planets, and so on. But of course by itself the complexity of a subject doesn't make it a science. Voodoo and witchcraft are also complex subjects.

And complexity, embellished by pseudo-scientific terminology, is just about all there is to astrology. The average person may fall victim to this glorification of astrology by its association with science, but not scientists. As they can now tell us, any vibrations issuing from the planets are negligible, if not unmeasurable— excluding, of course, the sun and moon, whose influences are measurable (for example, in the form of electromagnetic and gravitational effects). As Robert Morey points out in his excellent booklet *Horoscopes and the Christian*, a number of scientists have stepped forward to debunk the notion of planetary influences. In *The Humanist* Lee Ratzen claims that, according to his calculations, the doctor at the moment of an infant's delivery has a greater effect on the infant gravitationally and tidally than does the planet Mars. Carl Sagan, in his book *Other Worlds*, attests to the same fact (29-30). And finally, a Dr. Abell so forcefully states the case against "planetary influences" that he effectively silences all further debate on the matter:

> The tidal force produced on a man by the planet Mars when it is at its nearest to the earth is about 50 million times less than the tidal force on the same man produced by the typical Sunday copy of the *Los Angeles Times* lying on a table six feet away.
>
> —*Quoted in Morey 30*

Even if we acknowledge that electromagnetism and gravitation affect life on earth, astrological conclusions still aren't warranted. Dr. Percy Seymour, for example, maintains that solar activity affects the electromagnetic field that surrounds the earth and that this electromagnetic field affects us. Therefore, he believes that there may be some truth at the bottom of astrology after all, if all the layers of humbug are stripped away. But certainly even he must concede that any interactions between sun, moon, and earth would have to be so complex, so multifaceted in their effects that they would forever defy interpretive classifications. For every predictable phenomenon, there would be scores of seemingly random occurrences. Where predicting would be concerned, 100 percent, even 50 percent accuracy would be impossible. And here I'm only referring to natural phenomena. With humans, who interact by means of their free will with nature and other creatures, prediction would be all but impossible. Unless a person wants to deny free will, as behaviorists and genetic determinists do now, he must conclude that there will never be a perfect natural system that will explain human behavior or enable him to predict the future. And certainly modern-day astrology, based as it is on the "science" of ignorant ancients, is far from perfect.

Faced with scientific and rational refutations, astrologers, we might expect, would be silenced. After all, if planets don't shed vibrations that influence us on earth, then surely neither do the signs or constellations. But the star-gazers aren't as easily silenced as we might expect. When driven into a corner, they still have in their bag of tricks one more argument to which they appeal.

The Symbolic Truth of Astrology

As this book points out again and again, the last refuge of the New-Age theologian is subjectivism. And true to form, astrologers must finally appeal not to science or reason but to intuition. The signs and planets, they tell us, shed "spiritual influences" and represent "archetypal symbols" and "universal principles." Stephen Arroyo, an astrologer under whom I studied over twenty years ago, calls astrology "a *consciously usable mythology.*" "Whereas mythology," he claims, "places its emphasis on the cultural *manifestations* of the archetypes in various patterns, astrology utilizes *the essential archetypal principles themselves* as its language for understanding the fundamental forces and patterns in both individual and cultural life" (28ff.). In this way astrologers, besieged by science and religion, attempt to salvage whatever is left of their arcane pseudo-science by blending humanistic psychology, occultic abstractions, and miscellaneous mumbo jumbo. They succeed in convincing the naive by dazzling them with psychobabble and thus stunning them into agreement.

Yet we have a right to put the words of these humanistic astrologers to the test. What is the relationship between their "archetypal principles" and "the fundamental forces and patterns in both individual and cultural life"? Don't forces result in patterns, as when gravitation makes the apple fall from the tree? And aren't principles derived from the observation of patterns? We watch apples rotting on the ground, trees dying, and people aging and conclude that everything that lives must decay and die. Books on theoretical astrology are rife with this kind of bewildering language. Terms are loosely applied, categories are confused, and meaning is obscured. Evidently astrological writers and their readers aren't troubled by the confusion. They feel good about all their exploring, sharing, and experiencing—and that's all that really matters.

Even more to the point, can humanistic astrologers demonstrate any measurable correlation between real-life patterns and their principles? Can they verify that there is any causal relationship between real events—a laborer dropping a jackhammer on his foot, a child contracting the measles—and their "consciously usable mythology" consisting of various symbols—Mars, the god of war; Venus, the goddess of love; and so on? Because in fact these astrologers can't—and don't want to—provide any scientifically valid proof of such connections, they must at last take refuge in their ability to interpret horoscopes symbolically, to *intuit* the "universal principles" and to perceive "meaningful coincidences."

But what would even a 30 percent accuracy in their interpretations prove? Psychics, eyes closed, pieces of paper pressed against their foreheads, can do the same. So can certain shamans who read the entrails of animals or gypsies who read tea leaves. Faced with such difficulties, most astrologers end up enumerating the salutary effects that astrology has wrought in their lives, speaking about "psychic integration" and "holism." If it works for them, in other words, it must work. But personal testimony isn't a good defense for the validity of astrology. The palm reader, the witchdoctor, and the WICCA priestess can similarly claim that certain psychic benefits derive from the practice of their arcane arts. Who can argue with appeals to subjective experience?

Most practicing astrologers, however, aren't as intellectual as these humanistic astrologers, and yet they produce most of the astrological literature, the daily discardable stuff. As the following excerpt from a typical article in a local psychic newsletter illustrates, this literature is mostly fluff:

On January 1st, we begin the new year with *the third Saturn/Pluto square in the signs of Aquarius and Scorpio. This is a rare cycle* and has had an effect on us in 1993. *The square* denotes a time of change and brings to the forefront heavy issues that are wanting to surface in order that we might undo old patterns. It is a good idea to meditate and focus on healing family discord and deep-seated emotional traumas. *On January 11th, there will be a New Moon in Capricorn which creates a rare line-up of planets in . . .*

Capricorn: Sun, Moon, Mercury, Venus, Mars, Uranus and Neptune. This seems to be an incredible seeding and kick-off point for *the Uranus/Neptune energy* to begin to unfold and push forward a powerful time for illumination and insights. (italics mine)

Here we find a standard astrological preview of an upcoming month. Notice that at least a third of the passage consists of mere astro-babble, of no use to the uninitiated (as the italicized portions prove). Then consider the interpretation itself. Aren't all times times of change? Doesn't every period in life bring "heavy issues" to the forefront for anyone who walks, talks, and breathes? And in what sense can issues *want* to surface? Do issues have a conscious will of their own? Moreover, aren't all periods good for meditating, improving family relationships, and healing personal traumas? For those who are intent on growing spiritually, isn't every time good for illumination and the discovery of insights? On one level this passage tells us nothing; on another, it tells us what is already self-evidently true.

From my own years of experience as a former astrologer, I can say that the definitions of signs, planets, and houses overlap so much that astrology retains its aura of mystery—and in some circles its respectability—through its sheer vagueness. A perceptive astrologer, for example, can say the right things to his clients by simply observing their verbal and nonverbal cues. This client raises an eyebrow; that one sighs and leans forward. In response, the astrologer pursues the same line of interpretation or veers off in a new direction as he probes into his client's personal life and panders to his ego. Even when the client isn't present at the "reading," the astrologer can lapse into generalities that would be true of most people who seek help from astrologers: "You suffer from a deep dissatisfaction with yourself and life; for years you have felt insecure, unappreciated, but somehow certain that . . ." Or, "If you are attuned to the higher vibrations of your sign, you have felt an urge to . . ." Even given partial or inaccurate birth information, the "best" astrologers would be able to do a satisfactory job of interpreting a chart, proceeding as they do by vagueness and flattery and relying as they do on their much-vaunted intuitions.

Don't get me wrong. I don't believe that most astrologers consciously set out to deceive their clients, certainly no more than anyone else does who has a profit motive. Most of them, although very sincere, are simply self-deceived, having traded their critical faculties and objectivity for the joys of subjectivism—its certitude, its phony serenity, and its instant spirituality. All of us who sought spiritual enlightenment before coming to Christ can empathize with those who are tempted by the delights that astrology promises. A person in pain is like a person on fire—his first impulse is survival. Desperate and driven, he seeks the fastest and easiest way to put an end to his suffering. Upon this impulse astrology feeds because it promises a release from pain and an increase in self-esteem.

THE REAL NATURE OF ASTROLOGY

Even so, the effects of astrology on society and the individual are pernicious. As merely one more tool in the hands of New-Age teachers, it vigorously denies, or reinterprets, the truths of orthodox Christianity in order to advance the New-Age agenda. Christianity, the religion of the Piscean Age, New-Age prophets tell us, is simplistic and passé, and so it must be eschewed or reformed by the true seekers of the God Within. With our new awareness in the New Age, we are supposed to be able to control our own destinies and advance spiritually toward higher and higher states of consciousness. By understanding our birth charts in light of the so-called verities of astrology, we are supposed to be able to manipulate the energies shown therein—thus overcoming the root causes of our ignorance and karma.

Once again, the religion of the New Age—the way of self-reliance and self-aggrandizement—is being exalted—indeed, aggressively promoted—as the new and only true path to God, the impersonal Absolute of the yoga-Vedantins, who isn't a person but an abstract first principle toward which each soul is straining.

But as we have discovered, the entire foundation of New-Age theology is based on lies. Likewise, as this chapter demonstrates, astrology is a lie, and thus *the New Age itself is a fiction.* As understood by New-Age teachers and devotees, then, the New Age never was, nor will it ever be. The New Age is nothing more than a counterfeit of the new heaven and earth promised us by God in the Holy Bible, a book that unequivocally and uncompromisingly denounces astrology, divination, idol worship (including the worship of man and oneself), and spiritual pride. Tragically the unfortunate devotees of this false path and all its false messiahs have focused all of their attention not on God, but on a false Self whose inspiration is the life- and soul-destroying force behind New-Age theology: the angel of light, Satan.

Let those who have the ears to hear take heed. New-Age theology, in whatever guise it appears, is as deadly to the spirit as AIDS is to the body.

CONCLUSION

The Full
Armor of God

THE ROCK-LIKE PETER, WHO WAS CERTAINLY NO hysteric, delivered a significant warning to the Christians of the first century: "Be self-controlled and alert. Your enemy the devil prowls around like a roaring lion looking for someone to devour" (1 Pet. 5: 8). Still relevant in our own time—perhaps even more so because of the times in which we live—this warning should be taken as much to heart today as when it was written. Not only are unwary nonbelievers subject to attack, but so are Christians. Certainly the attack can come in dramatic ways, as when satanic symbols are spray-painted on a church building or when slanderous remarks are aimed at blameless, God-fearing Christians. More often than not, however, the attacks are subtle. Lions, remember, stalk their prey, crouching in the tall grass, shimmying along the ground on their bellies, before they charge and pounce.

As I hope this book has shown, New-Age terminology is one of the chief, most subtle means by which the enemy launches his assault. What is the difference between "Christ, the King" and "the Cosmic Christ," or between "the presence of God and Christ Jesus" (2 Tim. 4:1) and "Christ-Consciousness"? What is the difference between "salvation" and "liberation," or between "original sin" and "the law of karma"? The differences, as we know, are enormous. But it's through New-Age language that New-Age theology begins to gain credibility and even invade the Church. Some people begin to call Christianity "a path," and therefore other people presuppose, by implication, that there are other paths. Some people begin to call the Christian life "a journey," and other people assume that the Christian must get somewhere by dint of self-effort or a series of self-discoveries (rather than by means of self-sacrifice and God's self-revelation). Or some people speak of "getting centered in Christ," borrowing the word *centered* from yoga and Zen Buddhist practice, and other people assume that Christian sanctification involves using techniques to arrive at a desirable state of consciousness. As a result, the role of grace in the life of a Christian is minimized, and people outside Christianity begin to believe that Christianity is becoming more enlightened, more flexible, less doctrinaire.

But just as language use alters people's perceptions of Christianity, so does the consequent widespread acceptance of New-Age theology, aided and abetted as it is by the snippets of New-Age terminology appearing here and there. With new terms and ideas, people acquire and accept new assumptions without question. The average Joe or Josephine on the street begins to think in a new way. The post-Christian era in which we live gradually distances itself even more from Christianity. Without thinking, people say, "Man, that's bad karma." They begin to talk about "achieving wholeness" rather than "being saved." They deny that sin exists—and in fact dismiss the word *sin* with a kind of smugness and exaggerated revulsion. Instead, they say that the socially maladjusted are just "ignorant." Owing to the influence of reincarnation theory, people think of life as a kind of school. "We are here to learn lessons, and everything we do teaches us a lesson," they claim.

Nothing then is really sinful, if people have good intentions and in the end learn some lesson, preferably a "spiritual" one.

Now that people are supposed to have high self-esteem—and notice how easily the word *Self* can be substituted for the word *self*—they no longer need to feel shame. Moreover, because "all is one," people should be tolerant of all religious and moral differences and distinctions. And so it follows axiomatically that if there is no shame, there is no sin; if there is no sin (or absolute set of moral standards), there is no need of a salvation from sin; and if there is no need of salvation, there is no need of a Savior. And what is left of Jesus Christ? Only a smarmy, all-inclusive ascended master, only a generic, pseudo-mystical symbol of life, light, and love.

What can we Christians do in the face of this assault on the faith? Although an entire book could no doubt be written on the intelligent Christian reaction to New-Age theology, I will attempt a more modest undertaking in this conclusion. I will recommend a stance that I believe Christians should take in the face of New-Age theology and will encourage my readers to work out for themselves the details of their own responses to the New-Age threat. I will use the framework of Paul's well-known message to the Ephesians to elaborate on this stance:

> *Therefore put on the full armor of God, so that when the day of evil comes, you may be able to stand your ground, and after you have done everything, to stand. Stand firm then, with the belt of truth buckled around your waist, with the breastplate of righteousness in place, and with your feet fitted with the readiness that comes from the gospel of peace. In addition to all this, take up the shield of faith, with which you can extinguish all the flaming arrows of the evil one. Take the helmet of salvation and the sword of the Spirit, which is the word of God. And pray in the Spirit on all occasions with all kinds of prayers and requests. With this in mind, be alert and always keep on praying for all the saints.*
> *—Eph. 6:13-18*

May the following prayerfully written commentary help us all arrive at a prayerfully determined response.

THE BELT OF TRUTH

In the face of the evil that is upon us, Paul tells us that we must don the full armor of God by first putting on "the belt of truth." This "truth," of course, refers to the truth of the Gospel. But there is more to this advice than first meets the eye.

For the Roman soldier, the belt accomplished two things. First, it fastened his tunic in place. Without this belt, his loose tunic would have been appropriate for resting or lounging in his tent or home but not for fighting. In effect, he wouldn't have had his guard up. But with the belt, he would have been prepared to act. The bound tunic would have allowed him ease of movement, the ability to act quickly, to run, leap, engage in sword play. Second, it carried the scabbard that held his sword (Barclay 183). Without his belt, he would have been lolling about without his sword, unarmed, unprotected, yet comfortable.

For the Christian the message, I believe, is clear. He must be prepared at all times to defend his faith against demonic attack and to defend the faith itself. Where his faith is concerned, he must not rest. In practical terms, this "truth" that he has buckled onto himself must support and bear the Word of God, for Paul a few lines later in the same passage refers to the sword as the Word of God. To this end, a Christian must not only study Scripture daily but must also master Scripture as much as he is able. He should not only read Scripture to enhance his own life of faith but should also consult commentaries written by proficient, conservative scholars who fully accept the authority of God's Word.

Moreover, he must have a clear grasp of the essentials of the faith. Of course, he will try to understand the Trinity and the divinity of Christ, but he will also strive to understand and correctly employ such terms as *salvation, justification, atonement, sanctification,* and *glorification.* Only then, as a defender of the faith, will he have free movement within a dangerous, heretical world. Enjoying a degree of certainty and safety, he will find it impossible to compromise in the presence of danger or to flee from an attack.

As a result, when dealing with a New-Ager, the Christian will be alert, prepared, if necessary, for a loving confrontation. He won't have to shirk his responsibility. When the New-Ager haughtily asks, "What *is* sin?" the Christian who is informed about New-Age theology will be able to provide an answer: "Sin is wrongdoing, disobeying God and thus alienating oneself, through self-will, from God." If at this point the New-Ager claims that right and wrong are relative, the Christian may offer a challenge. "When is it ever right," the Christian might ask, "to sexually abuse a three-year-old child or to exterminate six million people because you don't like their ancestry?" In so doing, the Christian will get the New-Ager to admit that wrong does exist and that many acts, at least theoretically, are wrong always and absolutely. If the New-Ager demurs, claiming that he doesn't commit such gross wrongs against others, the Christian may then appeal to New-Age philosophy itself for support. According to the gurus, one's thoughts, words, and deeds must be pure if he is to make spiritual progress. Even impure thoughts—thoughts of hate or jealousy—generate bad karma and impede one's spiritual progress. Everyone, including this New-Ager, must therefore at some time be guilty of certain wrongs—or sins—against God.

The Christian might then proceed thus: "If one does wrong, any wrong at any time, one can't be perfect; so long as one isn't perfect, one can't 'become one with God.'" Even New-Agers will concede that "self-mastery" comes only to the perfect. Then for the Christian it's one short step to proving that no one can ever stop doing at least some wrong—that is, sinning—or, in a New-

Ager's words, "creating bad karma." Up to this point, even the gurus will agree, but they offer a different answer to the dilemma. "Escape from the endlessly turning wheel of karma," they say; "renounce and transcend the psycho-physical organism, and realize the True Self."

It's here, however, that the Christian, at last on familiar ground, can offer the New-Ager another answer to the age-old dilemma of sin, the Christian answer: "Jesus Christ alone, who loved us so much that he paid the penalty for our sins, can reconcile us with God once and for all. Not by self-effort, which continues to create good and bad karma, but only by faith in him alone can one be saved, freed forever from the 'law of karma.' Thereafter, a person embraces the world and his humanity, gratefully and willingly becoming a servant of Christ." At this point, the Christian will be equipped to answer for the New-Ager the hows and whys, referring to the deeds of Christ and citing Scripture (for example, John 3:16).

THE BREASTPLATE OF RIGHTEOUSNESS

While the Roman soldier was wearing a breastplate, a sword, dagger, or arrow couldn't pierce his heart or other vital organs. And, of course, if it was a breastplate only, it would have been of no use when he was retreating. But Roman soldiers didn't flee from battle unless they were willing to be ignominiously executed by their own officers. "We who are about to die salute you," they used to boast. They had only two choices before them: victory or death.

For a Christian, this breastplate is made of "righteousness"; indeed, it *is* his righteousness. What keeps the Christian from damaging his witness through hypocrisy, cowardice, and compromise? Wherever he goes, whatever he does, he holds to God's righteousness because it's the salvific love of Christ that has obligated him—indeed, has endued him with the power—to behave righteously. Inspired by Christ's great love for him, he is naturally a light unto others. He desires to do nothing that will bring shame to Christ. Because his righteousness is Christ himself, he will walk with Christ at all times and pray unceasingly. When coworkers tell dirty jokes, he won't participate or give his tacit consent by laughing along with them. If anyone is treated disrespectfully or unjustly, he will speak out. And always in showing responsibility and exhibiting self-control, he will be guided by faith and love (compare 1 Thess. 5:8).

The Christian will put his life on the line, not so much, in this case, to evangelize others, but to walk the Christian walk. Surely, because he isn't ashamed of the Gospel, he will speak at times about his Lord. But more importantly in this context, he will remain, as far as he is able and by the grace of God, blameless. Will he be perfect? No. But he will have enough humility to confess his shortcomings, seek forgiveness, and sincerely mend his ways. Even this stance shall bear witness to his faith. As the saying goes, "Christians aren't perfect; they are just forgiven." Nevertheless, the Christian who doesn't conduct himself righteously leaves himself and the Gospel open to attack—and that no self-respecting Christian should ever do.

In my experience, New-Agers, who generally respect earnestness and commitment, are impressed by a righteous—that is, a Christlike (not a self-righteous)—Christian. They have no trouble admiring and respecting a Dietrich Bonhoeffer, Albert Schweitzer, Corrie ten Boom, or Mother Theresa. A Christian's witness of faith, steadiness, peace, and love, therefore, is his best defense against the slings and arrows of skeptical, cynical New-Agers. When in the presence of a righteous Christian, a New-Ager must at least grant that Christianity is a "valid path." That concession can be the starting point for the Christian who is intent on sharing the Gospel—namely, "here is what we Christians believe and why we believe it."

THE SANDALS OF READINESS

The sandals of the Roman soldier enabled him to break camp quickly and to travel even to unknown barbarian lands. Could he leap up and quick-march at a moment's notice? Could he tramp over thorns or sharp stones? Certainly. Because the sandals protected the feet, they too, like the belt, allowed for freedom of movement. The soldier whose sandals were strapped to his feet would have been ready to follow orders, not in a few minutes after he found his sandals and then fastened them to his feet, but *immediately*.

According to Paul, the sandals of which he speaks give one "the readiness that comes from the gospel of peace." In the case of the modern Christian, he must be ready to spread the Gospel of peace—not just to exemplify it, but to proclaim it. Once again, in order to do so, he must understand the Gospel through his diligent study of the Scriptures. Even more importantly, however, he must be ready to carry the Gospel and bear witness to it anywhere. To do so, he should understand the terrain, the lay of the land.

In practical terms, he will be more effective as a witness if he understands the age in which he lives. True, his sandals will allow him to pass over any territory that he is called upon to cross, but if he is forewarned of the pitfalls and dangers, he will more deftly make his way across the wilderness of modern society as wise as a serpent, as gentle as a dove. And when he is spreading the Gospel, let him not forget Jesus' words: "If anyone will not welcome you or listen to your words, shake the dust off your feet when you leave that home or town" (Matt. 10:14). In this way, the Christian shouldn't allow himself to be troubled if people reject the Gospel of peace that he brings.

As a rule, New-Agers are impressed by that Christian who brings a Gospel of peace. They won't tolerate being harangued or lectured to by an agitated or overwrought witness. A

Christian, therefore, must himself display a peace that "transcends all understanding" (Phil. 4:7). If the Christian is patient, calm, sincere, humble, and, above all, loving, the New-Ager will be called to a higher standard of communication. He will have to respect the Christian who stands before him shod in the sandals of readiness. True, the Christian will be eager and enthusiastic, but he won't be pushy, aggressive, or unduly provocative. He will speak and respond gently but authoritatively, for he will know that his authority is the Gospel itself. Aided by the Holy Spirit, he will trust God for the words he will need to speak. And therefore he will be at peace.

THE SHIELD OF FAITH

With a shield, the Roman soldier would have been capable of parrying sword or spear thrusts aimed at his breastplate or head, holding his enemies at bay, or absorbing a volley of fiery darts (Barclay 183). In this way the shield-bearer enjoyed a measure of security. Without that shield the soldier would have faced almost certain death if two or more warriors fell upon him at the same time. And since a legion of soldiers advanced side by side, their shields held before them, they made a formidable, unstoppable phalanx.

Alone, to be sure, the well-outfitted Christian has his own formidable shield. Upon this shield, made of the most adamantine of substances—*sola fide*, faith alone, the cross of Christ is emblazoned. With it the believer can face any onslaught. Temptations and challenges, for such a person of faith, are blocked or deflected. The Christian must never forget that he has been saved—and is constantly being sanctified—by faith alone. Naturally this stance requires a growing trust as well. Having faith, he must trust that God will work all things for his good, making him a conqueror—not always over his opponents in the present, but definitely over death and the forces of evil in the long run. With faith he may fall in battle, but he will rise again, spiritually undamaged.

But perhaps the greatest strength is to be found in numbers, in an alliance of many faith-filled individuals within the Christian community. Informed, united believers, willing to advance against the chaos and the darkness, will pose the greatest threat to the purveyors of New-Age theology. To this end, Christians should oppose any watering down of the faith outside or inside the church. They can do so by mounting their own information campaigns. They can publish and distribute books and pamphlets on the dangers of New-Age thinking or take booths at psychic fairs or hold, for that matter, counter-psychic fairs. They must continue to make their presence felt in the news media, at school board meetings, and in the halls of legislatures.

Like the Roman shield, the most formidable defensive weapon in the ancient world, faith in Jesus Christ will protect Christians, even when New-Agers confront them. Every Christian will surely face some ridicule and rejection. But let him grasp the dimensions of his faith, the faith for which he stands, and persist in carrying it before him into the battle of life, fighting the good fight. Let him always be prepared to give an answer to everyone who asks him to give the reason for his hope, doing so with gentleness and respect (1 Pet. 3:15-16).

THE HELMET OF SALVATION

The Roman soldier's helmet was not only protective but definitive. Like the shield, the helmet protected the soldier's head from the blows that his enemies might inflict upon him. The soldier, having a helmet fitted snugly on his head and strapped tightly under his chin, would have had one more defense against attack and would feel all the more secure in his ability to ward off attacks. But consider also the appearance of the Roman helmet, with its bright red comb running from the forehead to the nape of the neck along the center ridge of the helmet, standing straight up like a stiff and brightly colored Mohawk haircut. Even from afar, no enemy could mistake the Roman soldier for any other. The enemies of these soldiers would know that they would soon be reckoning with the power of Rome. The helmet with its blood-red comb was a fearsome emblem.

In the same way, the Christian's salvation is also protective as well as definitive. First, it protects the believer's mind from attacks from without and within. Because the Christian always remembers that he has received his salvation by grace through faith, he can never boast of his own accomplishments or yield to persuasive appeals to his intellect. Whatever intelligence he has, he realizes, must remain informed by the Holy Spirit; howsoever capable his conscience may be, he seeks his authority in Scripture. If he is praised for his ability to share the Gospel, he won't swell with pride; if he is criticized, he won't lose heart. In short, he will possess discernment, placing all his faith not in the reasoned arguments and rationalizations of men (or his own mind), but in his continuing "hope of salvation" (1 Thess. 5:8).

Second, the Christian's salvation, like the Roman helmet, may also be regarded as a kind of emblem, an emblem of the shed blood of Christ. When the Christian declares that his salvation is based not on what he has done or can do but on what Christ has already done, he is making clear to others the source of his strength and authority. He is announcing his nonnegotiable, uncompromising position. All his thoughts and words must spring from this faith in the love and power of Christ. Only then will the witnessing Christian be unassailable and undefeatable.

How might this stance work in practice? Obviously, every Christian may not be capable of dealing with the hidden assumptions and slippery logic of New-Agers. But every Christian *can* wear and display his helmet of salvation. Consider this example. Let's imagine that a coworker has begun to wax eloquent about a forthcoming "harmonic convergence" that he wishes to attend.

"It's going to be held at the top of Mt. Shasta, which is a radiating center of power on the earth," he declares. The Christian might then ask, "What is the purpose of this meeting?" The New-Age proselyte will probably respond, "We're going to be sending out love to the earth in order to heal it." The fully-armored Christian could now cinch up his helmet strap and proceed. "I believe," he might say, "that a much purer, divine love has already been sent into the world and is there for anyone who asks for it. The supreme healer of all time, Jesus Christ, has already shown us how to heal not only the earth, but also the wounded people of the world."

What, then, can the New-Ager say? In speaking of the Savior, the Christian has exalted the one and only source of salvation. The New-Ager would then have to engage with the Christian or flee from any further discussion. Whatever then happens, the Christian has made his stand uncompromisingly clear.

THE SWORD OF HOLY SCRIPTURE

When dressed for battle, the Roman soldier could go nowhere without his double-edged sword, for it hung from the belt around his waist. And yet until an actual battle commenced, it remained in its sheath, always there as a lethal reminder to potential enemies that they should think twice before opposing the Roman army. At the same time, the sword wasn't like a Scud missile that could be programmed to do the attacking while the soldier who launched it sat back and waited for it to strike. The sword of the Roman soldier had to be wielded by the soldier himself. Standing toe to toe with his enemy, relying on the strength of his arms, he had to conquer the world for Rome or defend Rome against its attackers and invaders.

Likewise, the Christian must be prepared to wield the Word of God. Already, I have spoken of the Christian's need to be knowledgeable about the Scriptures. To be sure, the Christian

must be so equipped. But here I want to mention another neces-
sity. For the Holy Bible to retain its power and authority, its ability to penetrate into the hearts of others, it must be regarded by
every Christian to be inerrant. Any compromise, even saying that
the Bible is infallible in matters of faith and morals but fallible in
matters of historical fact, will dull its edge.

Who, after all, can really draw a definitive line between statements of fact and statements about faith and morals? Romans 1,
for example, unequivocally denounces homosexuality as being a
sin. But clearly, if modern scientific facts "prove" that homosexuals, because of the constituency of their hormones, have no
choice in the matter of their sexual preference, then factual-
minded folk would have to accept the homosexual lifestyle as
valid. The new *facts* would then have to supplant the old *moral
injunction* found in Scripture. Or because we have been enlightened by the feminists since the days when Paul advised Timothy
on the qualifications of pastors, we would have to conclude that
women today should be admitted into the ordained ministry. In
so doing, though, we would be disregarding the theological *faith*
of Paul.

Here again, are we dealing with facts or morals? Obviously,
with both. Those who compromise in this way end up on a slippery slope, sliding away from the Bible and landing in a ditch
wherein they have no recourse but to rely upon their own lights.
They become "tolerant" and thus water down the faith.

When New-Agers hear of Christian scholars and ministers
who question the reliability of Scripture, they are delighted. They
are confirmed in their own belief that Christ is a universal Savior
who would have eschewed all the doctrines, dogmas, and confessions that Christians, ever subject to the authority of Scripture,
still stand by today. "See," the New-Agers say, "the Bible-
thumpers can't thump their Bibles anymore." When Christian
scholars embrace the Gospel of Thomas, thumbing their noses at
canonicity, or when they question whether or not Christ even

spoke the words that appear in the gospels, they play right into the hands of the New-Agers.

One recent book, for example, entitled *The Five Gospels: The Search for the Authentic Words of Jesus,* has aroused much controversy in this regard (Lindelof A8ff.). After six years of work, a committee of seventy-four scholars, called The Jesus Seminar, has determined that Jesus didn't speak most of the words attributed to him in the gospels. And what have they concluded? After retaining only those statements that portray a wise but gentle, simple, and loving Jesus, they have concluded that Jesus was a "sage." New-Agers would love this appellation, for then Jesus would agree with all the "sages" the world over that love is the only answer to our spiritual and secular problems. Remember, "All you need is love, love; all you really need is love."

To keep the sword of the Word sharp, Christians must proceed on the assumption that the Holy Bible is absolutely trustworthy. True, at times they will disagree about certain fine points. But they must never disagree on the fundamentals, nor must they question the authority of the Bible within their own ranks or before the world. For if the Holy Bible isn't fully trustworthy, but instead is only partially trustworthy, if it only speaks to people "mystically" (or allegorically) but not practically, then the New-Agers will have no reason to alter their belief in the unity of all religions and the validity of all paths. Eventually nothing Christians say to them will carry any weight. Who, after all, will take seriously a paper sword?

THE POWER OF PRAYER

Finally, let's not forget that Paul concludes his message at the end of his epistle to the Ephesians by exalting the power and position of prayer in a believer's life. The full armor worn by the Christian isn't enough by itself. Because the Christian has at his disposal an even greater power—the power of the Spirit, he must pray "on all occasions" for himself and for others. Through prayer he receives God's protection; through prayer he remains in the service of Christ; through prayer he gains victory not only over principalities and powers (his true enemies) but also over all other forms of opposition. This is the power of the true kingdom, the Kingdom of God, that calls him into service and stands behind him. Through action borne of prayer, the Christian prepares the way for the coming of the Kingdom, and for this cause he is willing to die.

Prayer, then, is the Christian's most effective weapon against the advance of the New Age. By praying for strength and wisdom, while also lovingly praying for the salvation of every New-Ager he meets, the Christian will be doing his part. Prayer will fill him with grace, making him gracious and kind, and with the love of Christ, making him humble in spirit and committed to the cause of the Gospel. In this way the Christian will be prepared to participate, at a moment's notice, in loving confrontation with New-Age seekers and teachers alike.

Clearly, we Christians must adhere to certain nonnegotiable beliefs. Upon these we must take our stand. Prayerfully—living, moving, and having our being in the Spirit that guides us—we must be equipped to defend intelligently those beliefs and the faith from which they have sprung. There is no substitute for the preparation that comes from knowledge, for in this information age it is "knowledge" that is most often opposing us. In the face of such opposition, we can't afford to remain uninformed. The late C. S. Lewis stated this position well:

> If all the world were Christian it might not matter if all the world were uneducated. But as it is, a cultural life will exist outside the church whether it exists inside or not. To be ignorant and simple now, not to be able to meet the enemies on their own ground, would be to throw down our weapons and to betray our uneducated brethren who have no defense

but us against the intellectual attacks of the heathen. Good philosophy must exist if for no other reason than because bad philosophy needs to be answered.

—Lewis 28

Thus, what we need if we wish to reach New-Age seekers is knowledge—knowledge of our faith and of the world in which we now live.

For this reason, many traditional methods of evangelism—for example, slipping tracts under windshield wipers—probably won't move most New-Age seekers. Such people are too jaded and sophisticated to fall for what they perceive to be heavy-handed manipulation or appeals to "dogma." If we try to guide them through a series of simple questions and answers, they will merely recoil from us, thinking us unevolved and unenlightened.

On the other hand, if we rely instead on right reason, being informed and guided by the Holy Spirit and by Scripture, we will find ourselves in a more advantageous position. Now alert and flexible enough to meet them on their own ground, we will be capable of turning their own weapons, including words like "karma" or "Cosmic Consciousness," against them. Only when we are thus guided and equipped will we truly be able to say what needs to be said, when it needs to be said, to whom, according to the Holy Spirit, it needs to be said. We will then have put on the full armor of God.

Readers who wish to contact the author to discuss his experiences or arguments are invited to do so via his E—mail address: scott5@ix.netcom.com

WORKS
CONSULTED

Abhedananda, Swami. *Reincarnation*. 10th ed. Calcutta, India: Ramakrishna Vedanta Math, 1973.

Adams, Evangeline. *Astrology: Your Place Among the Stars*. New York: Dodd, Mead, and Company, 1933.

Albrecht, Mark C. *A Christian Critique of a New Age Doctrine: Reincarnation*. Downers Grove, Ill.: InterVarsity Press, 1982.

Anderson, U. S. *The Magic in Your Mind*. North Hollywood: Wilshire Books, 1979.

—— *The Secret of Secrets*. North Hollywood: Wilshire Books, 1977.

Arroyo, Stephen. *Astrology, Psychology, and the Four Elements: An Energy Approach to Astrology and Its Use in the Counseling Arts*. Davis, Calif.: CRCS Publications, 1975.

Ashtavakra. *Ashtavakra Samhita*. Trans. Swami Nityaswarupananda. 4th ed. Calcutta: Advaita Ashrama, 1975.

Avery, Jeanne. *The Rising Sign: Your Astrological Mask*. Garden City, N.Y.: Doubleday, 1982.

Bailey, Alice A. *From Intellect to Intuition*. 2nd paperback ed. New York: Lucis Publishing Company, 1974.

Barclay, William. Translation with commentary and interpretation. *The Letters to the Galatians and Ephesians*. Rev. ed. Philadelphia: Westminster Press, 1976.

Bhagavad Gita, The. Juan Mascara, trans. Baltimore: Penguin Books, 1962.

Bhartrihari. *Vairagya-Satakam or The Hundred Verses on Renunciation*. Swami Madhavananda, trans. 6th ed. Calcutta: Advaita Ashrama, 1971.

Blavatsky, Helena P. *The Secret Doctrine*. Los Angeles: Theosophy Company, 1925.

Brennan, J. H. *Five Keys to Past Lives*. New York: Samuel Weiser, Inc., 1971.

Bristol, Claude M. *The Magic of Believing*. New York: Pocket Books, 1948.

—— *TNT the Power Within You: How to Release the Forces Inside You—and Get What you Want!* Englewood Cliffs, N.J.: Prentice-Hall, 1954.

Brooke, Tal. *Lord of the Air: Tales of a Modern Antichrist*. Eugene, Ore.: Harvest House, 1990.

Carter, Charles E. O. *The Principles of Astrology*. Wheaton, Ill.: Theosophical Publishing House, n.d.

Case, Paul Foster. *The Book of Tokens: 22 Meditations on the Ageless Wisdom*. Los Angeles: Builders of the Adytum, 1978.

—— *The Tarot: A Key to the Wisdom of the Ages*. Richmond, Va.: Macoy Publishing Co., 1975.

Cerminara, Gina. *Many Lives, Many Loves*. New York: W. Sloane Associates, 1963.

——. *Many Mansions*. New York: New American Library, 1967.

Chakravarty, Sharat Chandra. *Swamiji's Message to a Disciple*. Calcutta: Advaita Ashrama, 1964.

Chidbhavananda, Swami. *Commentary on the Bhagavad Gita*. Madras, India: Sri Ramakrishna Math, n.d.

Darwin, Charles. *The Descent of Man and Selection in Relation to Sex*. Ed. Robert Maynard Hutchins. *Great Books of the Western World*. Vol. 49 Chicago:: Encyclopedia Britannica, Inc., 1952.

Davies, Dr. Ann. *This Is Truth About the Self: A Qabalistic Interpretation of the Pattern on the Trestleboard*. Los Angeles: Builders of the Adytum, 1974.

Emerson, Ralph Waldo. "Self-Reliance." Ed. Stephen E. Whicher. *Selections from Ralph Waldo Emerson: An Organic Anthology*. Boston: Houghton Mifflin, 1957.

Gammon, Margaret H. *Astrology and the Edgar Cayce Readings*. Virginia Beach, Va.: A.R.E. Press, 1973.

George, Llewellyn. *A to Z Horoscope Maker and Delineator*. St. Paul, Minn.: Llewellyn Publications, 1969.

Groothuis, Douglas. *Confronting the New Age*. Downers Grove, Ill.: InterVarsity Press, 1988.

—— *Unmasking the New Age*. Downers Grove, Ill.: InterVarsity Press, 1986.

Hall, Manly P. *Collected Writings: Essays and Poems* Volume 3. Los Angeles: The Philosophical Research Society, 1962.

Hunt, Dave and T. A. McMahon. *The Seduction of Christianity*. Eugene, Ore.: Harvest House, 1985.

Huxley, Aldous. *Collected Essays*. New York: Harper, 1959.

Jones, Marc Edmund. *Horary Astrology: The Technique of Immediacies, with a Primer of Symbolism*. Berkeley, Calif.: Shambala, 1975.

Kriyananda, Swami. *Your Sun Sign as a Spiritual Guide*. Nevada City, Calif.: Ananda Publications, 1971.

Leo, Alan. *How to Judge a Nativity*. New York: Astrologer's Library, 1978.

Lewis, C.S. "Learning in War-time," *The Weight of Glory and Other Addresses*. New York: Macmillan, 1949.

Lindelof, Bill. "Book Fuels Debate Over Jesus' Words." *The Sacramento Bee*. January 13, 1994.

M. *The Gospel of Sri Ramakrishna*. Trans. and introd. Swami Nikhilananda. New York: Ramakrishna-Vivekananda Center, 1969.

MacLaine, Shirley. *Out on a Limb*. New York: Bantam, 1983.

Maltz, Maxwell. *Psycho-Cybernetics*. North Hollywood: Wilshire Books, 1969.

Martin, Walter. *The New Age Cult*. Minneapolis: Bethany House, 1989.

Monks of the Ramakrishna Order. *Meditation*. London: Ramakrishna Vedanta Centre, 1972.

Morey, Robert A. *Horoscopes and the Christian*. Minneapolis: Bethany House, 1981.

—— *Reincarnation and Christianity*. Minneapolis: Bethany House, 1980.

Murphet, Howard. *Sai Baba: Man of Miracles*. Madras, India: Macmillan Company of India Limited, 1972.

Murphy, Joseph. *The Power of Your Subconscious Mind*. Englewood Cliffs, N.J.: Prentice-Hall, 1963.

Narayananda, Swami. *A Practical Guide to Samadhi*. 2nd rev. ed. Rishikesh, India: Narayananda Universal Yoga Trust, 1966.

Nikhilananda, Swami. *Vivekananda: A Biography*. 2nd Indian ed. Calcutta: Advaita Ashrama, 1971.

Nirvedananda, Swami. *Hinduism at a Glance*. 4th ed. Calcutta: Ramakrishna Mission Calcutta Students' Home, 1969.

Osborne, Arthur, ed. *The Teachings of Bhagavan Sri Ramana Maharishi in His Own Words*. 3rd ed. Tiruvannamalai, South India: T. N. Venkataraman, Sri Ramanasramam, 1971.

Paramananda, Swami. *Secret of Right Activity*. 4th ed. Cohasset, Mass., and La Crescenta, Calif.: Vedanta Centre and Ananda Ashrama, 1964.

Parkhurst, Louis Gifford, Jr. *The Believer's Secret of the Abiding Presence*. Minneapolis: Bethany House, 1987.

Peck, M. Scott. *People of the Lie*. New York: Simon and Schuster, 1983.

Ponder, Catherine. *Open Your Mind to Prosperity*. Unity Village, Mich.: Unity Books, 1971.

—— *The Prospering Power of Love*. Unity Village, Mich.: Unity Books, 1966.

Prabhavananda, Swami, and Christopher Isherwood. *How to Know God: The Yoga Aphorisms of Patanjali*. New York and Toronto: New American Library, 1953.

—— *The Sermon on the Mount According to Vedanta*. Hollywood: Vedanta Press, 1964.

—— *The Spiritual Heritage of India*. 2nd paperback ed. Hollywood: Vedanta Press, 1969.

Rajneesh, Bhagwan Shree. *The Mustard Seed: A Living Explanation of the Sayings of Jesus from the Gospel According to Thomas*. New York: Harper and Row, 1975.

Ramacharaka, Yogi. *Mystic Christianity or the Inner Teachings of the Master*. Chicago: Yogi Publication Society, 1935.

Ramakrishna, Sri. *Words of the Master: Selected Precepts of Sri Ramakrishna*. Comp. Swami Brahmananda. Calcutta: Udbodhan Office, 1970.

Rudhyar, Dane. *The Practice of Astrology: As a Technique in Human Understanding*. Baltimore: Penguin Books, Inc., repr. 1971.

Sakoian, Frances and Louis S. Acker. *The Astrologer's Handbook*. New York: Harper and Row, 1973.

Saradananda, Swami. *Sri Ramakrishna the Great Master*. Trans. Swami Jagadananda. 4th ed. Mylapore, India: Sri Ramakrishna Math, 1952.

Satprakashananda, Swami. *The Goal and the Way: The Vedantic Approach to Life's Problems*. St. Louis: The Vedanta Society of St. Louis, 1977.

"Sayings of Swami Vivekananda." Sacramento: Vedanta Society, n.d.

Seymour, Dr. Percy. *The Scientific Basis of Astrology: Tuning to the Music of the Planets*. New York: St. Martin's, 1992.

Shankaracharya, Sri. *Aparoksanubhuti or Self Realization*. Trans. Swami Vimuktananda. Calcutta: Advaita Ashrama, 1973.

—— *Crest-Jewel of Discrimination*. Trans. Swami Prabhavananda. New York and Toronto: New American Library, 1947.

—— *Self-Knowledge*. Trans. Swami Nikhilananda. 3rd ed. Madras, India: Sri Ramakrishna Math, 1967.

Shivananda, Swami. *Practice of Yoga*. Rev. 4th ed. Sivanan-dagar, Himalayas: Divine Life Society, 1970.

Stearn, Jess. *Yoga, Youth and Reincarnation*. New York: Bantam, 1966.

Stevenson, Ian. *Twenty Cases Suggestive of Reincarnation*. Charlottesville, Va.: University Press of Virginia, 1966.

Sutphen, Dick. *You Were Born Again to Be Together*. New York: Pocket Books, 1976.

Tester, Jim. *A History of Western Astrology*. New York: Ballantine Books, 1987.

Thorn, Sabina. *Precepts for Perfection: Teachings of the Disciples of Sri Ramakrishna*. Hollywood: Vedanta Press, 1961.

Three Initiates. *The Kybalion: A Study of Hermetic Philosophy of Ancient Egypt and Greece*. Chicago: The Yogi Publication Society, Masonic Temple, 1940.

Upanishads, The. Trans. Swami Prabhavananda and Frederick Manchester. New York and Scarborough, Ontario: New American Library, 1948.

Virajananda, Swami. *Toward the Goal Supreme*. Introd. Christopher Isherwood. Hollywood: Vedanta Press, 1973.

Vivekananda, Swami. *Inspired Talks*. Rev. ed. New York: Ramakrishna-Vivekananda Center, 1958.

—— *Jnana-Yoga*. Rev. ed. New York: Ramakrishna-Vivekananda Center, 1970.

—— *Karma-Yoga and Bhakti-Yoga*. Rev. ed. New York: Ramakrishna-Vivekananda Center, 1970.

—— *Raja-Yoga*. Rev. ed. New York: Ramakrishna-Vivekananda Center, 1970.

—— "Sayings." A single-page compilation. Sacramento, Calif.: Vedanta Society of Sacramento, n.d.

"Who." *Maha Yoga or the Upanishadic Lore in Light of the Teachings of Bhagavan Sri Ramana*. 6th ed. Tiruvannamali, India: T. N. Venkataraman, Sri Ramanasramam, 1967.

Williams, John K. *The Wisdom of Your Subconscious Mind*. Englewood Cliffs, N.J.: Prentice-Hall, 1964.

Yogananda, Paramahansa. *The Autobiography of a Yogi*. 12th ed. Los Angeles: Self-Realization Fellowship, 1990.

Yukteswar, Sri Swami. *The Holy Science*. 7th ed. Los Angeles: Self-Realization Fellowship, 1972.

INDEX

Abell, Dr., 180
Abhedananda, Swami, 11, 203
Acker, Louis S., 207
Adam and Eve, 65, 152
Adams, Evangeline, 203
Age of Aquarius, the, 24, 172, 173, 177, 178
Age of Enlightenment, the, 78
Akashic records, 140, 141, 142
Albrecht, Mark, 129, 203
Alpert, Richard, 11
Alpha Dynamics, 85
Anderson, U.S., 58, 203
Antichrist,the, 165
Aparoksanubhuti or Self Realization (Sri Shankaracharya), 207
Aquarian Gospel, The, 25
Aquinas, Thomas, 62
A.R.E., the, 93
Armor of God, the, 16, 187 (Conclusion *passim*)
Arroyo, Stephen, 182, 203
Ashtavakra, 203
Ashtavakra Samhita (Ashtavakra), 203
Astral projection, 91, 97
Astrologer's Handbook, The (Frances Sakoian and Louis S. Acker), 207
Astrology, 12, 24, 25, 59, 171 (Chapter 8 *passim*)
Astrology and the Edgar Cayce Readings (Margaret H. Gammon), 204

Astrology, Psychology, and the Four Elements (Stephen Arroyo), 203
Astrology: Your Place Among the Stars (Evangeline Adams), 203
Atman (the Self), 50, 51, 56, 57, 69, 70, 97
A to Z Horoscope Maker and Delineator (Llewellyn George), 204
Augustine, 41, 62, 173
Aurobindo, Sri, 13, 93
Autobiography of a Yogi, The (Swami Paramahansa Yogananda), 27, 208
Avery, Jeanne, 203

Baba, Meher, 93
Baba, Sai, 13, 27, 29, 30, 31, 93
Bacon, Francis, 172
Bailey, Alice A., 72, 89, 203
Barclay, William, 190, 203
Believer's Secret of the Abiding Presence, The (Louis Gifford Parkhurst, Jr.), 206
Bhagavad Gita, The, 11, 13, 29, 38, 56, 61, 66, 203
Bhartrihari, 203
Bible, the, authority of, 156, 190, 199
Blavatsky, Madame Helena P., 11, 89, 169, 204
Body, the, New-Age views of, 87, 88, 89, 90, 93, 94, 98, 100, 146 in relation to the soul, 99

"Book Fuels Debate Over Jesus'
Words" (Bill Lindelof), 205
Book of Tokens: 22 Meditations on
the Ageless Wisdom, The (Paul
Foster Case), 204
Brahman, 28, 29, 30, 50, 52,
53, 54, 55, 56, 57, 65, 66,
67, 69, 70, 71, 92, 93, 96,
145
Brennan, J. H., 204
Bristol, Claude M., 204
Brooke, Tal, 9, 31, 204
Brown, John, 50, 51
Buddhism, 13, 114, 159

Cabalism, 11, 58
Carter, Charles E. O., 204
Case, Paul Foster, 204
Cayce, Edgar, 24, 59, 89
Cerminara, Gina, 204
Chakravarty, Sharat Chandra, 97,
204
Channeling, 66, 96
Chidbhavananda, Swami, 56, 204
Christ Self, the, Christ-
Consciousness, 57, 114, 157,
158, 167
A Christian Critique of a New Age
Doctrine: Reincarnation (Mark
C. Albrecht), 203
Collected Essays (Aldous Huxley),
117, 205
Collected Writings: Essays and
Poems (Manly P. Hall), 72, 205
Commentary on the Bhagavad
Gita (Swami
Chidbhavananda), 204
Confessions (Augustine), 62
Confronting the New Age (Douglas
Groothuis), 166, 205
Conscious mind, the, 135, 137, 139
Consciousness, 37, 51, 55,
58, 68, 73, 79, 91, 92, 94,
102, 104, 105, 107, 108,
132, 146, 153, 162, 164,
165, 185, 188
Copernicus, 171
Course in Miracles, A, 71
Creation, nature of, 56, 68, 112
real or illusion?, 56, 65

Crest-Jewel of Discrimination (Sri
Shankaracharya), 69, 70, 88, 207

Darwin, Charles, 109, 133, 204
Dass, Ram, 11 see also Richard
Alpert
Davies, Ann, 58, 68, 76, 105, 204
De Chardin, Teilhard, 25
Deism, 78
Deity, nature of see God, nature of
Demons see Evil spirits
Descent of Man and Selection in
Relation to Sex, The (Charles
Darwin), 204
Devi, Sarada, 23
Devil, the, Satan, an angel of light,
18, 155, 169, 170, 186. 187 see
also Evil spirits
Dewey, John, 109
Divine Light Mission, The, 93
Dreams, dream symbols, 97, 136,
137
Drugs, 25, 120
D'Souza, Dinesh, 101
Dualism, 29

East-Indian philosophy, Eastern
philosophy, 10, 11, 12, 13, 45,
48, 68, 69, 72, 73, 109, 111
Eckankar, 93, 161
Eliot, T. S., 28, 41
Emerson, Ralph Waldo, 11, 33,
106, 111, 159, 204
Evil spirits, angels of light, 131,
169, 170
Experience, 66, 92, 99, 103, 104,
105, 106, 119, 129

Faith, as a weapon, 189, 195, 196,
199
Fillmore, Charles, 68, 93
Five Gospels: The Search for the
Authentic Words of Jesus, The,
200
Five Keys to Past Lives (J. H.
Brennan), 204
Four Quartets (T. S. Eliot), 41
From Intellect to Intuition (Alice A.
Bailey), 203
Freud, Sigmund, 109

Gammon, Margaret H., 60, 204
Gauguelin, Michel, 171, 172
George, Llewellyn, 174, 204
Gestalt therapy, 97
Ginsberg, Allen, 11
Gnosticism, 10, 59, 90, 149
Goal and the Way: The Vedantic Approach to Life's Problems, The (Swami Satprakashananda), 207
God, nature of, 44, 56, 64, 65, 81, 83, 123, 146
  New-Age views of, 15, 25, 51, 52, 61, 62, 63, 68, 70, 71, 72, 80, 92, 115, 152, 161, 186
  personal, 43, 92, 93
  seen as impersonal, 52
God-consciousness, 18, 22, 67, 87, 94, 96, 98, 102, 160
Gospel, as a weapon, 189, 190, 193, 194, 195, 197, 201
Gospel of Sri Ramakrishna, The (M.), 205
Grace, 14, 48, 75, 81, 82, 83, 103, 104, 125, 146, 153, 160, 188, 193, 197, 201
Groothuis, Douglas, 9, 166, 205

Hall, Manly P., 71, 89, 205
Harmonic convergences, 173
Hegel, Georg Wilhelm Friedrich, 109
Hermes Trismegistus, 61, 73
Hermeticism, 10, 59, 61, 78
Higher Power, the, 52, 76, 95, 96, 97, 98, 100, 105, 108, 116
Higher Self, the, 51, 59, 60, 93
Hill, Napoleon, 97
Hinduism, 13, 14, 21, 28, 29, 31, 35, 68, 72, 89, 94, 101, 112, 116, 129, 158, 159, 171, 175
Hinduism at a Glance (Swami Nirvedananda), 206
Hippocrates, 171
History of Western Astrology, A (Jim Tester), 171, 207
Hitler, Adolf, 102
Hobbes, Thomas, 109
Holy Bible see *Word of God*
Holy Science, The (Sri Swami Yukteswar), 208

Horary Astrology: The Technique of Immediacies, with a Primer of Symbolism (Marc Edmund Jones), 205
Horoscopes and the Christian (Robert A. Morey), 180, 205
How to Know God: The Yoga Aphorisms of Patanjali (Swami Prabhavananda and Christopher Isherwood), 71, 206
How to Judge a Nativity (Alan Leo), 205
Hubbard, L. Ron, 60
Humanist, The (Lee Ratzen), 180
Hume, David, 109
Hunt, Dave, 205
Huxley, Aldous, 11, 119, 205

Ignorance, substituted for sin, 15, 68, 81, 90, 103, 107, 108, 111, 117, 152, 185, 188
Illusion, 22, 65, 68, 69, 70, 87, 91, 95, 99, 101, 108, 124, 152, 153, 155 also see *Maya*
India, 12, 13, 14, 51, 109, 110, 145, 165
Inerrancy of Scripture, the, 199, 200
Influence of the planets, the, 173, 179, 180, 181, 182
Inner child, the, 161
Inspired Talks (Swami Vivekananda), 82, 105, 110, 113, 116, 208
Isherwood, Christopher, 11, 71, 206

Jainism, 13
Jnana-Yoga (Swami Vivekananda), 208
Jesus Christ, true view of, 43, 44, 45, 46, 123, 125, 146, 147, 148, 153, 154, 161, 167, 168, 169, 170, 193, 197
  New-Age views of, 25, 50, 51, 86, 108, 120, 150, 153, 155, 156, 158, 166, 167, 168, 170, 189, 200
Jesus Seminar, The, 200
Jones, Marc Edmund, 205

Kant, Immanuel, 109, 121
Karma, 12, 15, 52, 55, 67, 68, 73,
    74, 75, 76, 77, 79, 81, 82, 83,
    86, 91, 101, 102, 103, 104, 107,
    113, 132, 133, 137, 140, 142,
    143, 145, 152, 153, 160, 162,
    163, 164, 165, 185, 192
Karma-Yoga and Bhakti-Yoga
    (Swami Vivekananda), 116, 208
Kepler, Johannes, 171, 172
Koresh, David, 115
Kriyananda, Swami, 205
Kundalini, 37, 72, 96
Kybalion: A Study of Hermetic
    Philosophy of Ancient Egypt and
    Greece, The (Three Initiates), 73,
    207

Letters to the Galatians and
    Ephesians, The (William
    Barclay), 203
Leo, Alan, 205
Leviathan (Thomas Hobbes), 109
Lewis, C. S., 201, 202, 205
Liberation, 67, 71, 94,101, 122,
    147, 162, 164 also see Mukti
Lindelof, Bill, 200, 205
Locke, John, 141
Lord of the Air, The (Tal Brooke),
    31, 204
Luther, Martin, 123, 146

M., 47, 70, 112, 205
MacLaine, Shirley, 60, 205
McMahon, T. A., 205
Magic in Your Mind, The (U. S.
    Anderson), 58, 203
Magic of Believing, The (Claude M.
    Bristol), 204
Maharshi, Ramana, 13
Maha Yoga or the Upanishadic
    Lore in Light of the Teachings of
    Bhagavan Sri Ramana Maharshi,
    208
Maltz, Maxwell, 205
Many Lives, Many Loves (Gina
    Cerminara), 204
Many Mansions (Gina Cerminara),
    204
Martin, Walter, 9, 205

Maya, 30, 52, 65, 67, 68, 69, 70,
    77, 81, 95, 97, 111, 137, 164
Meditation, 22, 56, 88, 98, 99,
    145, 152, 161 also see TM
Meditation (Monks of the
    Ramakrishna Order), 205
Merton, Thomas, 46
Mill, John Stuart, 109
Mind control, 86, 96
Mithraism, 10
Monism (non-dualism), 52, 53, 55,
    56, 62, 69, 70, 89, 111
    qualified, 53, 54, 55, 56, 59, 60
    strict, 57, 65
Monks of the Ramakrishna Order, 205
Montgomery, Ruth, 24
Morey, Robert A., 129, 180, 205
Mueller, Max, 11
Muktananda, 93
Mukti, 71
"Multicultural Reading List, A,"
    101
Murphet, Howard, 205
Murphy, Bridey, 130
Murphy, Joseph, 79, 206
Mustard Seed: A Living
    Explanation of the Sayings of
    Jesus from the Gospel According
    to Thomas, The (Bhagwan Shree
    Rajneesh), 206
Mystic Christianity or the Inner
    Teachings of the Master (Yogi
    Ramacharaka), 89, 206

Narayananda, Swami, 206
Neo-Platonism, 10, 11
New Age Cult, The (Walter
    Martin), 205
New-Age theology, see especially
    10, 16, 17, 18, 52, 58, 68, 77,
    87, 105, 107, 109, 115, 128,
    129, 150, 155, 160, 165, 166,
    167, 168, 169, 186, 188, 196
New Thought, 57
Newton, Sir Isaac, Newtonian
    physics, 78, 172
Nietzsche, Friedrich, 102, 109
Nikhilananda, Swami, 206
Nirvedananda, Swami, 206
Non-dualism see Monism

On Christian Doctrine (Augustine), 41
Open Your Mind to Prosperity (Catherine Ponder), 61. 69, 206
Order of the Adytum, the, 93
Orphism, 10
Orthodox Christianity, 10, 75, 124, 153, 157, 160, 161, 166, 167, 169, 185
Osborne, Arthur, 206
Other Worlds (Carl Sagan), 180
Ouspensky and Gurdjieff, 93
Out on a Limb (Shirley MacLaine), 205

Pantheism, 12, 56, 70
Paramananda, Swami, 206
Parkhurst, Louis Gifford, Jr., 206
Patanjali, 13, 27, 88
Past-life recall, readings, memories, 59, 91, 97, 127, 129, 130, 131, 132, 136, 137, 138, 139, 140, 141, 142, 143, 144
Peace of mind, 91, 94
Peck, M. Scott, 168, 206
People of the Lie (M. Scott Peck), 169, 206
Piscean Age, the, 25, 160, 173, 185
PMA (positive mental attitude), 62
Polarity therapy, 97
Ponder, Catherine, 61, 69, 206
Power of Your Subconscious Mind, The (Joseph Murphy), 206
Prabhavananda, Swami, 49, 50, 54, 71, 206
Practical Guide to Samadhi, A (Swami Narayananda), 206
Practice of Astrology: As a Technique in Human Understanding, The (Dane Rudhyar), 207
Practice of Yoga (Swami Shivananda), 207
Prakriti, 68, 71, 72, 73, 77, 81
Prayer, as a weapon, 189, 193, 200, 201
Precepts for Perfection: Teachings of the Disciples of Sri Ramakrishna (Sabina Thorn), 207

Pride, 93, 104, 108, 186
Principles of Astrology, The (Charles E. O. Carter), 204
"Proof-texting" by New-Agers, 74
Prophet, Elizabeth Clare, 89, 93, 113, 169
Prospering Power of Love, The (Catherine Ponder), 206
Psycho-Cybernetics (Maxwell Maltz), 205
Ptolemy, 12, 171
Pythagoras, 171
Pythagoreanism, 59

Raja-Yoga (Swami Vivekananda), 208
Rajneesh, Bhagwan Shree, 93, 206
Ramacharaka, Yogi, 89, 149, 112, 206
Ramakrishna, Sri, 11, 22, 23, 30, 33, 35, 37, 38, 41, 43, 44, 45, 47, 70, 82, 92, 93, 95, 111, 112. 206
Ramakrishna Order, the, 22, 23, 31, 36
Ramanuja, 54
Ratzen, Lee, 180
Readiness, the weapon of, 189, 194, 195
Real/unreal, the, 70, 87, 97, 111
Reichean therapy, 97
Reincarnation, 12, 15, 25, 74, 99, 127 (Chapter 6 *passim*), 150, 188
Reincarnation (Swami Abhedananda), 203
Reincarnation and Christianity (Robert A. Morey), 129, 205
Relativism, relativity, 41, 65, 78, 101, 105 (Chapter 5 *passim*), 147, 155, 156, 157, 191
Religion, 49, 50, 51, 90, 93, 112, 113, 114, 115, 116, 189, 200
Religious Science, 57
Renunciation, 22, 23, 39, 90, 97, 99, 114
Righteousness, the weapon of, 189, 192, 193
Rising Sign: Your Astrological Mask, The (Jeanne Avery), 203
Robbins, Anthony, 60

Rolfian therapy, 97, 161
Rosicrucians, the, 93, 129
Rousseau, Jean Jacques, 109
Rudhyar, Dane, 174, 207
Russell, Bertrand, 109

Sagan, Carl, 180
Sai Baba: Man of Miracles
 (Howard Murphet), 205
Sakoian, Frances, 207
Salvation, 103, 125, 146, 153, 154,
 157, 173, 189, 196, 197, 198
 as a weapon, 189
Samsara, 67, 70
Saradananda, Swami, 207
Sartre, Jean Paul, 109
Satan see Devil, the
Satchitananda, 93
Satprakashananda, Swami, 57, 73,
 207
"Sayings of Swami Vivekananda,"
 33, 207, 208
Science, and the New Age, 12,
 78, 130, 135, 171, 172,
 173, 179, 180, 181, 182,
 183
Scientific Basis of Astrology: Tuning
 to the Music of the Planets, The
 (Percy Seymour), 207
Secret Doctrine, The (Madame
 Helena P. Blavatsky), 204
Secret of Right Activity (Swami
 Paramananda), 206
Secret of Secrets, The (U. S.
 Anderson), 203
Secular humanism, 162, 168
Seduction of Christianity, The
 (Dave Hunt and T. A.
 McMahon), 205
Selections from Ralph Waldo
 Emerson: An Organic Anthology
 (ed. Stephen E. Whicher), 204
Self-effort, 86, 91, 123
Self-Knowledge (Sri
 Shankaracharya), 207
Self-realization, 15, 18, 57, 88, 160,
 162, 163, 165
"Self-Reliance" (Ralph Waldo
 Emerson), 107
Self-Realization Fellowship, The, 11

Self-will, a New-Age virtue, 90, 91
Sermon on the Mount According to
 Vedanta, The (Swami
 Prabhavananda and Christopher
 Isherwood), 49, 206
Seymour, Percy, 171, 172, 181, 207
Shankaracharya, Sri (Shankara), 27,
 53, 69, 70, 71, 88, 207
Shivananda, Swami, 13, 74, 83,
 207
Shruti, the, 66
Sikhism, 13
Sin, 102, 125, 160, 188, 189, 191.
 192
Skinner, B. F., 109
Smith, Houston, 11
Spiritual evolution or advancement,
 53, 75, 86, 87, 89, 91, 100, 102,
 120, 132, 133, 134, 135, 141,
 161, 163, 168, 185
Spiritual Heritage of India, The
 (Swami Prabhavananda and
 Christopher Isherwood), 54, 206
Sri Ramakrishna the Great Master
 (Swami Saradananda), 207
Stearn, Jess, 24, 207
Steiner, Rudolf, 25
Stevenson, Ian, 130, 207
Subconscious mind, the, 73, 96,
 135, 136, 137, 138, 139, 140,
 141, 142
Subjectivism, 66, 99, 100, 104,
 105, 106, 107, 108, 109, 111,
 116, 117, 118, 121, 122, 123,
 124, 147, 150, 156, 160, 161,
 181, 185
Summa Theologica (Thomas
 Aquinas), 62
Sutphen, Dick, 207
Swamiji's Message to a Disciple
 (Sharat Chandra Chakravarty),
 204
Swami S., 21, 22, 29, 31, 32, 33,
 40, 81, 112, 158

Tarot: A Key to the Wisdom of the
 Ages, (Paul Foster Case), 204
Teachings of Bhagavan Sri Ramana
 Maharishi in His Own Words,
 The (Arthur Osborne, ed.), 206

Tester, Jim, 171, 207
Theosophy, 11, 59, 93, 129
Think and Grow Rich (Napoleon Hill), 97
This Is Truth About the Self: A Qabalistic Interpretation of the Pattern on the Trestleboard (Ann Davies), 204
Thoreau, Henry David, 11, 50
Thorn, Sabina, 207
Thoth, 171
Three Initiates, 61, 73, 207
TM (Transcendental Meditation), 161
TNT the Power Within You: How to Release the Forces Inside You—and Get What you Want! (Claude M. Bristol), 204
Toward the Goal Supreme (Swami Virajananda), 208
True Self, the, 15, 51, 56, 57, 81, 89, 91, 93, 96, 102, 103, 105, 107, 108, 116, 144, 152, 153, 164, 192 see also *Higher Self*
Truth, 47, 66, 68, 70, 103, 104, 105 (Chapter 5 *passim*), 156, 157 as a weapon, 189, 190
Twenty Cases for Reincarnation (Ian Stevenson), 130
Twenty Cases Suggestive of Reincarnation (Ian Stevenson), 207

Unity School of Christianity, 57, 68
Universe, nature of the, 87
Unmasking the New Age (Douglas Groothuis), 205
Unsolved Mysteries, 129, 130
Upanishads, The, 13, 49, 52, 53, 54, 55, 56, 57, 60, 66, 83, 87, 101, 112, 207
Vairagya-Satakam or the Hundred Verses on Renunciation (Bhartrihari), 203
Vedanta, Vedantins, 12, 13, 22, 32, 36, 37, 39, 43, 45, 111
Vedanta Society, the, 21, 22, 23, 31, 32, 33, 36
Vedas, the, 13
Vegetarianism, 94

Virajananda, Swami, 208
Visualization, 91, 96, 100
Vivekachudamani (Shankara), 27
Vivekananda, Swami, 11, 13, 23, 33, 82, 105, 110, 111, 113, 116, 117, 208
Vivekananda: A Biography (Swami Nikhilananda), 206

Weight of Glory and Other Addresses, The (C.S. Lewis), 205
Western Occultism, 10, 11, 14, 24, 56, 57, 64, 66, 72, 86, 91, 92, 96, 112, 129
Whicher, Stephen E., 204
WICCA, 12, 159, 183
Williams, John K., 61, 83, 208
Wisdom of Your Subconscious Mind, The (John K. Williams), 208
Word of God, as a weapon, 189, 190, 198, 200
Words of the Master: Selected Precepts of Sri Ramakrishna (Sri Ramakrishna), 206
Wordsworth, William, 27, 41

Yoga, 12, 13, 22, 53, 56, 88, 94, 98, 161, 188
bhakti yoga, 29, 38, 97, 98
hatha yoga, 59, 93, 94
jnana yoga, 29, 37, 97, 98
karma yoga, 29
raja yoga, 29, 96
Tantric yoga, 72, 113
Yoga Aphorisms, The (Patanjali), 27
Yogananda, Swami Paramahansa, 11, 13, 27, 93. 208
Yoga-Vedanta, yoga-Vedantins, see especially 12, 13, 49, 51, 52, 53, 56, 59, 81, 83, 90, 98, 110, 111, 122, 124, 141, 186
Yoga, Youth and Reincarnation (Jess Stearn), 207
Your Sun Sign as a Spiritual Guide (Swami Kriyananda), 205
You Were Born Again to Be Together (Dick Sutphen), 207
Yukteswar, Sri Swami, 94, 208

Zen Buddhism, 161, 188
Zodiac, the, 172, 173, 174, 175,
   176, 177, 178, 179